# The Entrepreneur

## Volume Two

# *The Thrill of the Ride*

# Hans Sitter

King's Publishing

The Entrepreneur: Volume Two: The Thrill of the Ride

©Copyright 2017 by Hans Sitter

Books may be purchased by contacting the publisher or author at: info@KingsbBiergarten.com.

Published by

King's Publishing
1329 East Broadway St., Pearland, TX 77581

Cover and Interior Design: Nick Zelinger, NZ Graphics
Editor: John Maling (Editing By John)
Manuscript Consultant: Judith Briles (The Book Shepherd)

Library of Congress Cataloging in Publication Data

ISBN: 978-0-9862427-3-1 (Hard Cover)
ISBN: 978-0-9862427-4-8 (Soft Cover)
ISBN: 978-0-9862427-5-5 (eBook)

1) Business    2) Entrepreneur    3) Memoir

First Edition Printed in the USA

To Tony Robbins,
Megan, and my son, Philipp

CHAPTER

1

# My Early Childhood

*Why was all this happening to me?*

My mind was spinning as I tried to erase the picture in my head of my son, Philipp, kicking and screaming in his mom's arms, as they were leaving the Monaco airport. I was crying helplessly now, leaving my old world and life and on my way to Houston and a new life. As usual, my wife Karin had made herself up like a model, dressed in a short outfit, as though she was headed out for a date.

Fortunately, on looking out the airport window, I was able to get my last glimpse of Philipp, now walking next to her and our faithful dog, Umberto, on her other side. In my mind, I took that picture as I flew to my new and unknown destiny.

When we reached altitude, I rang for the stewardess. I wanted, no I needed, two Jack Daniels and two Cokes.

My eyes were red and swollen from crying. When she brought me the drinks and a cup with ice, she asked, "Are you okay, sir? Do you need anything else?"

"Could you bring me a mask? That would be appreciated."

"Certainly," she replied. A couple of minutes later, she returned with the eye mask.

I poured the whisky over the ice and then the Coke and took a big gulp. Putting on the mask, I felt for the next 12 hours—until we arrived in Houston—that I would be free of distraction. But I was not really tired; I couldn't sleep. Too much had happened. Dozens of thoughts were flying through my head. Trying to calm down after the stress of leaving my family and home, I began to organize my thoughts.

Why was my life always such a big drama, a constant roller-coaster ride?

Why was I under such extreme tension?

Why did I attract people like "Linkov" and other con artists?

Why was all this happening to me?

Could it really be bad luck—coincidence—or was it my screwed up personality, my character, my personal "Law of Attraction?"

None of my real friends or family had that kind of roller coaster life, with such extreme ups and downs. What had happened to me?

I started to think about my past. My thoughts returned to the restaurant of my parents, to my brother and the little town where I grew up.

I closed my eyes and saw myself as a very young boy playing and always laughing. Focusing on those memories, the vision became clearer and clearer and I fell into a trance. My mind flew away as I transported myself into my past.

I believe my childhood was fairly normal. At least in my eyes, it wasn't't bad at all. I went to school with my brother, Franz, and academically, we both did pretty well, but we never had the same interests or friends. The truth was, I hated most of his friends. As a kid, I loved to sit in one of our large trees in the garden behind the restaurant, hiding in the branches behind the thick leaves. Whenever his friends came over, I practice shooting at them with my sling shot. I got really good at it—not that it made Franz all that happy.

I spent a lot of time in the trees. I connected them with boards and mounted a railing made of steel pipe on either side of each board. So then I could run from one tree to another, holding the pipe for balance. My fantasy was in between swinging on vines like Tarzan and having a real tree house among those huge branches.

Before my brother and I were born, my parents bought a German Shepherd to protect our restaurant, and, when I was older, Ponto became my best friend. The two of us were inseparable; I don't know who loved the other more. After all, he was with my brother and me since we were born.

But Franz never played with Ponto. On the other hand, sometimes I even slept with him in his dog house. When I think about those times, I can't help but smile.

Sure, my brother and his friends thought I was a strange kid, but at least they left me alone and I was happy in my own, mostly private, world.

Both Franz and I had to work, even when we were still in primary school. We came home from the school around 1:00 PM and had to hop into our uniforms and start serving drinks and food in the restaurant.

Of all the challenges I had as a child, one influenced my character the most. It was my size—I was a bit smaller and thinner than my classmates. Also, my brother—two years older and about a foot taller—towered over me, as did his friends. It may seem like an exaggeration, but I felt I lived in the Valley of the Giants.

Smaller people, however, often assume certain defense mechanisms to deal with what they perceive as a disability. In my case, living in a world of aggressive and often cruel boys, I assumed the outlook best summed up as "attack is better than defense."

I learned this from a little terrier I had observed once. He compensated for his small size by jumping into the fray even before it started. His perceived lack of strength or smallness was overcome by an immediate and extreme attack.

If someone started a fight with me, even just hesitantly started to push me around, he quickly found himself embroiled in the "real deal."

Attacking first takes the wind out of bullies, who mostly enjoy the foreplay before the fight convinced they will surely win. No one bullying me had the luxury of more than a few moments to experience that pleasure—I was all over him before he even thought of throwing the first punch.

But outside of that unerring tendency to attack first any potential assailant, my life otherwise was pretty much normal ... except for one—constant work.

When our friends went with their parents on vacation during school break, my brother and I had to service the lunch crowd in the restaurant. Not only couldn't we go on vacation, we couldn't even go to the public pool like the kids who had to stay at home. Yes, we had time to play with our friends—after work—

but not much. As far as I remember, we never went with our parents on vacation.

Although life doesn't always hand you what you want, it sometimes gives you surprising gifts. I am quite sure my ability to work hard and steadily, sometimes without a break for an extended period of time, has fueled my ability to stay in the entrepreneurial game, sometimes winning millions at the roulette table in life's casino.

As John Paul Getty said, "After I work seventeen hours in a row, I begin to get lucky."

My entrepreneurial education did not have much to do with school, and I doubt school is the proper platform for this important skill, even today. It took place in a real family restaurant, where Mom was the cook who labored with only one helper, a lady who cleaned the dishes and even lived with us as a family member. Dad acted as the bartender and, alongside Franz and me, as waiter.

On Sunday, we closed at 2:00 PM and every Monday was a day off. Every Sunday at 9:00 AM, my brother and I went to church. My parents were committed members of the Catholic Church and my brother and I were honored to serve as altar boys, which earned us our parents' respect and approval. Religion was a thing highly valued in our community and it was more or less accepted by us as a natural and unquestioned way of life.

We were fortunate enough to have a public cinema in our town. Each Sunday, right after church, its doors were thrown open from 10:30 until noon, just for a kid's movie or a cartoon. The movie cost only one schilling—about five cents.

Like clockwork, we had lunch at home promptly at 2:00 PM And every Sunday, it was the same: wiener schnitzel and potato salad.

Wiener schnitzel in Austria means a thin slice of pork coated in breadcrumbs and fried. Meat was still rare and expensive in the sixties, even fifteen or more years after World War II. It was a treat for our week of hard work.

I had to smile as I thought about our living circumstances at the time. We had no shower or a real bathroom. Instead, we had a wooden bathtub. Every Saturday afternoon, Mom would heat up water on the stove and we had to take a bath in the restaurant's kitchen. It may not have been as appreciated as wiener schnitzel on Sundays, but Franz and I accepted it as our lot.

Having since owned and run steam rooms, whirlpools and saunas in gymnasiums, it makes me laugh to think how certain activities are regarded as added luxuries of life, to be savored and enjoyed, whereas, hot baths back then were more like a grim necessity to us.

Cars were another thing. They were absolutely coveted.

My father got his first car when I was six years old and it was a sensation. At that time, 80 percent of Austria was totally "car-challenged." They were few and far between.

Four years later, when I was ten, we got our first black and white television. It had only one channel—but again, our family was ahead of the curve. However, in regards to acquiring even basic technology, we were more than ten years behind the States, and, even when it happened, our technology was not nearly as good.

It is unbelievable how the times have changed. When I try to remember my childhood, it seems like I am already a hundred years old, the gap between the lifestyle then and now is so tremendous. Has all this really happened in just one lifetime?

Until now, on my flight to Houston, I never really thought about my past so clearly. I was always very busy with the "right now." But later on, in the 1990s, when I endured the trauma of losing all that I owned and had worked for as well as everything that was dear to me, this retrospection became the key to rebuilding my life. I needed to understand what had led me to such enormous wealth, and then to such frequent failures, the latest of which culminated in the loss of all my assets as well as my family.

HIGH OVER THE ATLANTIC, I HAD TO REFOCUS ON MY PAST BECAUSE I DIDN'T WANT TO REPEAT— BUT MY FUTURE WAS UNCERTAIN.

At this point, high over the Atlantic, I had to refocus on my past because I didn't want to repeat—but my future was uncertain.

I asked myself how I built myself and my fortune to such an extent that I could live and fluidly interact with the Super Rich and the celebrities in Monaco, and then dive into the pit of financial nothingness—almost in a heartbeat—right at the cusp of having just made three million dollars? It was not the most money that I had ever made, but it was certainly a very fat chunk.

When thinking about my childhood in post-war Austria, I realized that the clues to acquiring enormous wealth, which I have experienced on more than one occasion, lay right there when work was almost all we did and was the center of my childhood existence.

## 2

# End of Childhood

*I loved playing with the horses and working a big tractor.*

Remember how I said that the restaurant was closed on Mondays? Did you think that meant that we actually had a break from work?

Nope. As soon as we came home from school on Monday, we ate a quick lunch and then were driven to nearby Oslip, located in Burgenland, a little village with a population of about 1,200, to help my grandfather bottle wine.

Grandpa, my mother's father, was a multi-faceted entrepreneur. Among other commercial properties, he had grape vineyards from which he made wine for his own use, and for my family to sell in their restaurant. He never charged Mom and Dad for the wine. His goal was to help support them and their restaurant. All our family had to do was bottle and haul it to the restaurant.

Arriving at Grandpa's place every Monday, we'd head downstairs to the wine cellar and extract the wine from big, wooden barrels. We were allowed to bottle and take 30 two-liter bottles of red wine and the same of white wine. While we were bottling the wine, my mom was busily cooking dinner upstairs for all of us.

Grandpa's two Haflinger horses were used for working the vineyards and his tractors for the fields were very big in those days. Smaller tractors did not even exist then.

I loved playing with the horses and working a big tractor—that was exciting for me.

While Grandpa was an important part of our lives, unfortunately I don't remember my grandmother very well. All that I would recall when I tried to recapture my memories of her was that she was a very quiet person.

My father's dad also lived in Oslip, but he died when I was two years old. On his way home from work, he was riding a bicycle when he was hit by a truck. After his death, his wife, my other grandmother, continued to live in Oslip with her daughter. And my father's other sister, Aunt Agnes, and her husband, Uncle Franz, also lived there.

The family was a bit confusing when I was growing up. Mom's brother was also named Franz and his wife was also named Agnes. That Uncle Franz ran the restaurant and the butcher shop in Oslip. Things can get a bit crazy when you have two uncles named Franz and two aunts named Agnes living in the same village.

My father's sister had two kids, a boy and a girl, Ludwig and Wilma, who were my cousins. Ludwig was my age, but his sister was four years older. Dad's brother was a priest and missionary in Lima, Peru. He also was a Professor in Lima at the University of Santo Toribio de Mogrovejo and at the University La Pontificia Universitad Catolica. His kids, my cousins, went to a Swiss international school, Colegio Pestalozzi, and afterward they studied at the Universidad del Pacífico.

My family has a "history" like many families. When I was growing up, some sad things happened. Mom's brother, Uncle Franz, and Aunt Agnes had one child who died at only three days old. They weren't able to have any more children after that. They never got over it; in effect, it shattered their marriage.

Franz's wife, Agnes, started to sleep with various and sundry customers she met at the restaurant. Uncle Franz started to drink heavily, sometimes even clueless as to his wife's behavior, who, practically in his presence, would act like a common whore.

One year after she had begun her campaign of self-destruction, Franz died at forty-two of liver disease from his drinking.

Now, my maternal grandfather (my mother's father) in the tradition of many Austrians who trusted their children, had given all his property to his son, Uncle Franz (my Mom's brother) prior to his death. Under certain circumstances it was common in Austria, but not common in the United States. In return, it was expected that his son would care for his mother and him along with my grandparents for the rest of their natural lives.

Franz' sudden death meant that, legally, my Aunt Agnes, notwithstanding her strange behavior, now fell in line to inherit all the properties, including the restaurant, the butcher shop, the vineyards and everything else my mother's father had worked for his entire life.

After her death, the estate would normally pass to my brother and me, since Agnes and Franz had no children of their own.

But instead of using the properties to make a living for herself, she immediately put everything on the market for sale.

My grandfather was heartbroken.

He could not believe what she was doing, which was sabotaging the plan for his estate, a plan intended to take care of himself, my grandmother and our family.

Grandpa tried to negotiate with her, telling her that it would not be right to sell everything, but she told him that she didn't "give a shit" whether it was fair or not. She wanted the money so she didn't have to work anymore.

He immediately decided to buy everything back, but did not have enough cash to buy back all the properties.

What he did do was buy back as much as he could. He got back the restaurant, the butcher shop, eight wheat fields, six vineyards and the forest. In the end, my aunt got a great deal of cash from my grandfather, and still had six vineyards and five wheat fields to sell.

After that deal, grandfather was mentally and financially broken. He now realized that he had made the biggest mistake of his life, giving everything to his son before he died. But it was too late now to do anything about it.

Soon after he bought back a good part of his estate from my aunt, his wife died. After losing his son and my grandma and having to deal with the consequences of dealing with my aunt, he was a beaten down man. He had fought in World War I and World War II and managed to survive, but the loss of his immediate family and control over his own estate was the final straw. Six months later, he followed my grandma. He was 83 when he died.

My parents then inherited everything that he had bought back, and they leased the Oslip restaurant and collected $800 in rent every month.

When I was twelve, I was struck with a facial paralysis. I was playing soccer with my friends. Although it was springtime in Austria, it was unusually cold that day. Soccer can be a very vigorous, demanding sport, and that day I began to sweat profusely in the cold air. An icy wind came up, giving me a terrible chill, yet I did not stop. I kept kicking and running and yelling to my team mates, giving it my all.

The next morning, I awoke to find that the right side of my face was paralyzed. The feeling was strange as hell. In the mirror, I was horrified to see that my right lip was hanging down, and my right eye was wide open and seemed incapable of closing. I looked like Frankenstein or some god-awful zombie, a refugee from one of those 1940s horror movies. When I tried to yell for help, I found I couldn't move my lips, and even if someone could hear, no one could understand what I was saying.

DURING MY ENTIRE CHILDHOOD, MY MODUS OPERANDI WAS TO ATTACK FAST AND HARD AT THE SLIGHTEST PROVOCATION.

Dad went to the hospital with me, and I was immediately referred to a specialist, probably a neurologist.

Following that visit to the doctor, I had to wear a stocking cap day and night to keep my head warm at all times. I also had to cover my eye during the entire day and night. During the day, I wore a blindfold over the bad eye. Because I could not close my eye, the doctor was trying to make sure that my eye would not dry out, making it vulnerable to infection.

With the stocking cap, the eye patch and the blindfold, I looked like a pirate from the Caribbean. Everyone I talked to was distracted and alarmed by my appearance.

As many people experience when they have an unusual malady, I had to go through a lot of medical procedures as the doctors experimented with me to try and restore the function of the nerves in my face.

After many failures, a doctor was found who had the right approach. He administered electroshocks to my face to jump-start the nerves. The procedure was unbelievably unpleasant and I screamed and cried every time he put me through this painful ordeal.

Pre-adolescent kids can be particularly brutal, and they made every effort to bully me during this time. My face and the way I dressed ignited their laughter and derision but that proved to be more their problem than mine. I didn't make it easy on any of them, particularly if they laughed at me during school.

During my entire childhood, my modus operandi was to attack fast and hard at the slightest provocation. This was originally because of my size, but now it was about my appearance that caused them to focus on humiliating me.

It didn't take long. After a few weeks of this, these little bullies learned the slightest smile could start a fight, and I was fighting them constantly. Yes, I was small, but I was tough, and although not strong I was superfast. When I walked by a crowd of kids, there was silence—not a trace of joking or jeering.

Soon, I became an object of fear, not derision. Kids that had felt my wrath physically stayed as far away as possible. I was now treated with respect no matter how I looked. My terrier mentality had succeeded.

I DECIDED TO TAKE ON THE
WORLD AND NOT RETREAT,
NO MATTER WHAT.

Despite the electroshocks, I never healed completely, and even today you can see a tiny bit of paralysis in my face. Eventually, I got used to it.

But although I had eliminated the bullies in my life, I was still handicapped in regards to dealing with the young girls I wanted so badly to impress. I couldn't get to know them because of my appearance and manner. I was deeply hurt inside as a result.

When I talked to anyone at that time, I would cover my mouth when I talked, particularly when I tried to smile. I looked at myself as hopeless and ugly, and, until very recently, I didn't regard myself as handsome in any way. I had a real complex.

After many years of researching my problem, I learned that my condition is called Bell's Palsy or Facial Paralysis. Had the electroshock treatment been started immediately, it could easily have been completely fixed. But when nerves governing the movement of the body—in my case, the muscles of the face—don't get immediate treatment, they die quickly and cannot be restored or regrown.

Having Bell's Palsy was horrible for me. In reality, it's a terrible handicap for any sensitive young kid. Instead of retreating into a hole and hating myself, I applied the same strategy to my life that I applied to bullies, namely, attack is better than defense. I wished this challenge had never been present in my life, yet in hindsight, it did have a powerful effect on my development of character.

I formed a strong will to make something out of my life, to get the attention I felt I needed from my peer group and society at large and to be successful, whatever it would take. I decided to take on the world and not retreat, no matter what.

As you will see from my story, this attitude saved my life, my personal wealth and my ability to have strong, interpersonal relationships throughout my life. I would ultimately face the challenges that can only confront a real risk taker—I learned to be able to take my life on directly, no matter what the handicaps I faced. After reaching the eighth grade, my parents first asked my brother, Franz, "What do you want to do ... do you want to go to college or do you want a profession?"

My brother said he didn't want to go to school. Two years later, it was my turn, "What do you want to do ... do you want to go to college or do you want a profession?" I immediately said I want to learn to become a butcher. As you remember, I was always smaller than the other kids, and I was convinced that when I would work as a butcher, I would become big and strong.

At that time there was no education about body building nor were there fitness centers such as we have today. Rumors were told about butchers. Everyone believed that they drank raw blood! That was the reason they became so strong and big. And that was my primary reason to choose the vocation of a butcher. A second reason was that I hated to ask for every penny from my parents. I wanted to enter the working class as fast as possible and generate my own income. My brother was assigned the task of learning to be a full-time waiter and I was learning the fine art of butchering meat.

The plan was clear. My brother would eventually take over the restaurant in Wiener Neustadt, population 50,000, and I would take over the restaurant and butcher shop of my grandparents in little town of Oslip, population 1,200.

My parents warned my brother and me many, many times to think carefully about our decisions, but neither of us wanted to study any longer. Because of this decision, one I made so early on, I had to learn everything in my life the hard way.

At the tender age of 15, I had to leave home and "work my butt off" ... just like an adult. I was given my schedule, the schedule to begin my life as a butcher.

I would start working at 3:00 in the morning and work through the day until 4:00 in the afternoon. My apprenticeship was monotonous and grueling, largely confined to making sausages and killing all kind of animals. After working for thirteen hours with just a lunch break, I was allowed to rest for a few hours.

Rest meant sleep, the sleep of the truly exhausted kid, but only for two hours. I had to get up at 6 PM to clean the retail shop, about an hour's task. Then, I ate and had to go straight to bed in order to rise again at the early hour of 3 AM.

I thought about the words of my parents, to think twice about either going to school or choosing to work. It was too late to change my mind then. I never wanted to be a quitter.

For efficiency's sake, I slept where I worked, in a tiny attic room in the butcher shop. I was only allowed to go back to see my parents in Wiener Neustadt on Sundays.

I was too proud to quit, but often when watching my friends who had selected to go to college, I asked myself why I had chosen this life instead. What the hell was I thinking ... what was I doing?

To fully prepare me for my future vocation, I worked on Saturdays behind the counter in the butcher shop. We closed at noon and then my free time started.

Saturday afternoon until three Monday morning.

One day, my parents called to say that Ponto, my German Shepherd and best friend, had died. This was a great tragedy for me.

Hearing the news, I immediately stopped working and returned home. There, I walked through the restaurant to the garden in the back, where I began to dig a grave for my dear companion. The grave was beneath one of the large trees and, after I finished, I cried for several hours. As I looked around at the trees surrounding the grave, I could see myself happily running from tree to tree on the boards, quicker than a speedy squirrel, with Ponto running on the ground below, following my every movement, barking and wagging his tail with excitement. He had been a great friend all during my early years, guarding me against danger and taking part in all my solitary childhood pastimes. But now he was gone.

CHAPTER

3

# Waking Up Briefly

*I was ready for another whisky.*

I felt tears as I awoke from the recollections of my childhood. I wasn't sure where I was momentarily. I took off my eye mask, lifted my head and looked around, and recognized reality.

I was ready for another whisky before going back to my journey into the past and rang for the stewardess who promptly appeared saying, "It looks like you're feeling better, sir."

I said, "Yes, but I will feel even better if I can get another double whisky." She smiled and asked, "Another Coke too?"

"No thanks, I still have Coke."

I finally took a closer look at the lady next to me and saw how beautiful she was. A couple of minutes later I received my whisky and made my mix, took a big gulp again, stretched a little bit and looked once more at my beautiful neighbor, who was reading a journal. I thought I should try to talk to her, but then decided to put my mask back on and return to my travel into the past.

CHAPTER

4

# Branching Out

*I learned about the real business world*
*at The Airport Bar.*

After my best friend was buried, I had to return to work the next day. It was as though nothing had happened. It was hard for me to believe. I recognized that it was the way life was. When you were dead, you were gone—gone forever. And I had to get my ass back to work.

For all this work, I only got $20 a week—not really a lot, not even in those days. And, for sure, it was not enough for me.

So to make more money, I found work as a disc jockey in a bar and discotheque. It was called Café ERIKA and I worked Saturday from 7 PM until 2 AM then on Sunday from 5 PM until 10 PM. For those two days, I received $80, quite a bit of money for me at the time.

On Sunday, after work, I usually stayed up until midnight at the bar with our customers, who would often buy me drinks and invite me to sit and talk with them.

A number of self-employed business people used to hang out and spend a lot of money there. I learned about the real business world at that bar.

One customer was a young guy named Tony Zach. He had a tire shop that he ran with his father, and from all the money he was dropping in the bar, it seemed to me he was pretty wealthy. Every time he came into the disco, I greeted him conspicuously on the microphone, often choosing songs that I knew he especially liked.

Over time, despite the fact he was ten years older, we became good friends. He was a kind of role model for me, someone I would like to be like when I was his age.

Another customer I met in the disco was a guy named Ferrence Barat. He was Tony's age and he dealt with diamonds, which he brought from Antwerp and Amsterdam. He also had a package delivery company. As a hobby, he collected antiques. Ferrence was a very metropolitan guy and smart, but also very strange and complex.

I LEARNED ABOUT THE REAL BUSINESS WORLD AT THAT BAR.

Another favorite visitor to the "Meeting Point" was Hans Holz. His father owned The Airplane Bar, which was located on the highway on route to Vienna. It was across from a vocational school and close to the airport in Wiener Neustadt.

Hans spent also a lot of time and money at the Café ERIKA. He was only two years older than me, unlike many of the other older guests, and I talked to him frequently. He had a gorgeous girlfriend and I liked to watch them dance together. Their rock n' rock moves and symmetry were so freaking perfect. I admired them and created a real nice friendship.

In Austria you can drink alcohol when you are 16 and nobody ever asks for proof of age. But got my first hangover way before I was 16.

Yes, the disco and my job there was great. The bad side of my story is that when I left the club Sunday at midnight, my workday as a butcher started on Monday at 3 AM. I maybe got two hours of sleep if I was lucky.

For the entire Monday, I was ridiculously tired. I had to struggle through the day not to fall asleep. Life was really tough back then.

After three years of this schedule, I took an examination and became a fully licensed butcher.

When I was eighteen years old, I also acquired my commercial driver's license, allowing me to drive vehicles that included limousines, taxis and large trucks.

In my mind I was ready to take on the world, ready to move forward. My dreams were big and I felt invincible.

## CHAPTER

# 5

# The End of Butchering

*But in this moment I knew: that was not my future,*
*that was for damned sure!*

After I got my license, I moved immediately to Vienna where I lived with my cousin, Ludwig, in his apartment. He studied economics at the University of Vienna, and I worked in the meat department of a supermarket chain.

That was a big jump in my career. Now I was making $2,000 monthly, a pretty good salary in 1971 for someone my age.

While at a friend's birthday party, I met my first real love, Herta. I was 18; she was 16. Soon I was happily in love.

My used Mini Cooper set the stage for our first sex adventure. The car was small and the logistics were not exactly made in heaven, but by the time we finished, we were happier than when we started. However, my first thought afterward was: Is that it? Is that all?

I expected so much more from sex. It was not bad, but not so great either.

I really didn't know what I expected but the more I thought about it, it was for sure ten times better than a jack-off and the after feeling was relaxing. The pressure was gone, and it was a pretty cool feeling in my head.

In the supermarket, I had to deal with the supervisor of the meat department. He was a freaking asshole, but I was making $2,000 a month. I thought that dealing with him was the price and sacrifice I would have to make to go further, professionally.

Every Monday fresh meat—pig carcasses—was delivered in a huge refrigerator truck.

From where the truck parked to the cold storage locker where the pigs to be processed were stored was at least 400 feet away. We worked there in the cold chill of the morning, mist still rising from the damp street. The truck driver stood on the trailer and carefully loaded the pigs onto my shoulder, one by one. I guessed that there were around 60 to 80 half pigs that I was to carry the long way to the cold storage ... those 400 miserable feet.

I started to carry the pigs while Fred, the supervisor, and various workers stood around, smoking and chatting. From the very beginning, I could not stand the guy, but I had made my decision; I told myself to ignore him and just do my work. As I passed by Fred, he made smart ass comments like: "Can you handle it, buddy?" Then with a big smile on his face, he said, "You're a strong boy. You can do it."

Supervisor or not, I wasn't afraid of him, and I was in no mood that morning for his words. My thoughts were: *Listen, Fred, you'd better leave me alone. I don't need any of your snide comments when I'm working and you're doing nothing.*

As I pushed my way into the cold storage freezer, reaching high above my head, hanging one pig after another on hooks that reached down from the ceiling, I became more and more resentful of their refusal to help me with the huge job.

The morning wore on as I carried one carcass after another, watching my coworkers as they dragged on their cheap cigarettes and hurled mocking comments at me.

"Come on, kid, you can do it ..." they tossed out as they stood around, smiling and chatting with each other like old women, laughing at my expense.

That day I had carried around 25 pigs to the freezer, one by one, each spread heavily across my shoulders for the long, 400-foot walk to the cold storage. I was tired—worn out—each pig heavier than the last. It was as if my shoulders were laden with granite. With the next pig I carried, I stopped, looking around at the insanity of my life at this moment and the scene in front of me. My head suddenly spun with the thought that a bunch of idiots like these would get paid to do *nothing*, and I, who had worked every moment of my life since I was eight years old, would have to answer to *them* ... it was too much to bear.

Without moving on, I arrogantly dropped the pig in front of them. *Whoops, I'm so sorry I interrupted your little party, Fred. But maybe that gives you something to do.*

The pig slid a few inches on the damp ground where they stood and landed squarely on Fred's foot.

Fred's eyes grew large and he started screaming hysterically at the workers around him, kicking the pig off his foot. He yelled at them to grab it—pick it up—get it off the ground. They struggled and tried in vain to pick up the pig, but it was slippery and slid away from them, twisting on the ground that was now like a slop-enhanced sty. I stood there in my frustration and anger watching Fred's merry band of idiots struggle. Fred started to scream at me for

> "LISTEN ASSHOLE, I'M NOT YOUR SLAVE."

dropping the carcass, but I was already at the bitter edge from enduring their endless insults, my body sore from carrying carcass after carcass all morning. The scene swam before me. I listened to Fred's screaming voice and "saw red."

Blind with anger, I turned and I grabbed him by the throat, pressing him so hard against the wall that he could barely breathe. Fred broke free and tried to pull a butcher knife from its sheath on his belt, but I slammed his hand hard against the wall and he dropped it. Regaining my hold, I pressed him back into the wall and leaned all my weight against his throat.

Close enough to smell his rancid cigarette breath, I said slowly, "Listen asshole, I'm not your slave. Nobody in my adult life ever laughed at me, and you're not gonna' be the first and get away with it. Do you get it?"

Fred tried to nod, but my grip on his throat made it impossible.

"Start up with me once more and you'll never bother anyone again in your lifetime." My tough guy persona was expressing itself fully.

My coworkers surrounded us by then, as Fred tried to escape. Nobody really tried to help him, though. I looked at them and sneered, dropping him to the ground. Then, for some reason, I walked into the cutting area.

The cutting area was a room with a huge wooden table where the pigs were cut into parts. The table was covered with mounds of pig parts—shoulders, legs, a huge pile of ribs, and finally, at the far end, pork heads.

Something snapped in me that cold morning unloading pig carcasses as I left Fred crumpled and gasping for air and made my way to the filthy cutting room. The long table of pigs' heads, in my imagination, seemed to be leering at me, laughing.

What I was doing there that day was the next step in my training—working at a "good" job as a butcher with a supermarket chain. It was a good salary, with great benefits. And I'd been told that after working there for a few months, I would be able to get a general manager position in a meat market—a coveted position. *This was supposed to be success? But in this moment I knew: that was not my future, that was for damned sure!*

Insanely, I began throwing pork heads, one after another across the room. Then I took a pork leg and wielded it like a samurai sword. I ran with the pork leg in my hand through the room, striking two large hall stands that flew through the room and crashed onto the floor.

Still running with the pork leg, I rammed it into a nearby shelf resulting in a loud crash from pieces of shattering glass and porcelain mugs as they flew everywhere. I covered my eyes as shards hit my face, and I started bleeding.

As I raced by a mirror, I was astounded to see myself. I was a crazed Viking warrior racing into battle with his swine leg axe! I stopped, frozen, and looked at myself and started screaming at my image. "Sure this is the perfect job—working with idiots and being treated like shit. Screw this!"

I hit the mirror with the swine leg-slash-axe, and the mirror broke into hundreds of pieces. I wasn't finished yet! The rage at Fred, his posse of idiots—and even at myself and my life—surged out of me. I went to a shelf where the knives were stored, took one knife after another, and threw them at two half-pig carcasses hanging on the nearby wall.

Each time a knife landed in a pig carcass, it made a grotesque sound, and soon the pigs looked like porcupines in a Frankenstein movie.

I looked around at the carnage and screamed again as loud as I could. "Is this what it's all about? Is this all there is? This is my dream? What was I thinking, working my ass off for three years so I can butcher some stupid pigs!"

Finally, I stopped. I was exhausted and breathing heavily. Two women from the delicatessen department of the supermarket came into the room. They stood there—mouths open and in shock—viewing the destruction that I had caused with my frenzied outburst.

I turned to them, screaming, "Get OUT, out of here, damn it. Leave me ALONE!"

They had no reaction, standing there frozen, just looking at me. I raised my pork leg over my head and rushed toward them. And then they ran screaming from the room.

Not sure what to do next, I picked up my bag of personal belongings and left the room just as Fred came in and saw the carnage.

"You're going to regret this, Sitter!"

"Screw you, Fred," I said, pushing him out of the way. "You better get away from me or you will regret it." I tromped through the glass and debris, turning back as I left. "Oh, and by the way ... I quit, asshole!"

CHAPTER

6

# Another Supermarket ...
# and Selling Auto Parts

*I would make two thousand bucks in profit with one hit.*

Just one week later I found a new job in another supermarket, and after a long interview I became the manager in that market! It was much smaller, but at least I did not have to deal with a "fucking asshole" like Fred.

The general manager from the market was a nice guy and we got along from the first day. His name was Gerald and he was funny, very smart and I respected him. He introduced me to a lot of people and after work, I began to moonlight by trading and selling all kinds of auto parts: radios, spark plugs, batteries, used alternators, etc. By the time I was nineteen, I was making $2,200 at my job and at least $3,000 on side auto part deals. This was a lot of money for someone my age.

One day a guy came to me and asked for 2,000 spark plugs. Without blinking an eye, I said, "No problem. You can pick them up in two days."

I got in touch with my delivery guy, who worked in car parts in the main warehouse of a big chain, and he also delivered parts to the market where I was working. He also was a good friend of Gerald, my general manager. He brought me the spark plugs the next day.

I would make two thousand bucks in profit with one hit, a really good deal for me. I was very happy. Now, all I needed was the buyer to come pick them up.

He came two days later to pick up the plugs. After I gave him everything he ordered, he replied by showing me his badge.

This was not good was the first thought shooting in my brain .

He turned out to be an undercover officer who promptly arrested me. I was shocked. I asked him why?

As he slapped the handcuffs on me, he said simply, "For selling stolen goods. Don't you know?"

From the moment we began to drive to police headquarters, nothing I said mattered. I asserted again and again my innocence. I knew nothing about it. There was no evidence that the spark plugs were dirty. I had often worked with the delivery guy and I thought everything was on the up and up. I begged, I pleaded, I cajoled, but it was as though I didn't exist. He listened, but didn't say a word until we pulled up in front of a very large and dark building.

"You are going to be put in jail until they clear your case, period. Now shut your trap," he said.

CHAPTER

7

# Jail Time

*It was like a lottery for criminality, a total nightmare
for a young, inexperienced business person like me.*

According to what I learned as the charges were rolled out against me, this was a pretty big bust. A lot of people were involved, and there were a lot of arrests. These people were working in the same warehouse as my delivery guy, and the fact was, they stole the parts and sold them to people like me. The question was, was my delivery guy part of the "gang"?

That was the first time I had the distinct honor of appearing in the newspaper—with a headline, no less! It cleverly said:

BETWEEN HAM AND SAUSAGE – CAR PARTS

The article began with, "Butcher Johann Sitter is selling stolen car parts in a supermarket chain."

That article brought both of my parents close to a heart attack. Such events are greatly magnified when you live in a small town like Wiener Neustadt.

I distinctly remember my father visiting me with Herta. I looked at them from the other side of the glass window and tears were running down my face as I tried very hard to play the tough guy.

Herta looked at me and put her hands on the window, coming as close as she could to touch and comfort me, but the glass panel is made to augment emotional isolation—and it worked. As she reached toward me, I could clearly see tears in my father's eyes.

Eventually, when I calmed down, we spoke over the microphone. My Dad told me he would look for a lawyer, which he did.

When they left, I was not really heartened. When you see people you love and you can't even touch them, the disconnect from home, family and friends is heightened and the emotional pain is even greater. I prayed that they would get me out as soon as possible. Even though I had not done anything intentionally, I was not exactly comforted about what I had seen so far about the justice system. Later on in my life, this impression would be increased a thousand fold.

If I was dismayed by the justice system itself—the system of arrests, interrogation and courtroom procedures—I was even more appalled, even terrified, by the prison system.

I had to spent three weeks in jail with twenty other people in the same cell. This wasn't the usual crowd I was used to, even though I worked in a bar where there were a lot of strange people who were pretty free with their money and seemed to associate with suspicious-looking friends. Probably some pimps, high rollers and white collar criminals, no one typically very violent, but there had been a few menacing scenarios from time to time. But it was nothing like the cell I was confined to.

THE WORST PART OF THIS EXPERIENCE FOR ME WAS NOT THE CRIMINALS, THE DRUNKS, OR THE SKIRMISHES. IT WAS THE TOILET.

It was like a lottery for criminality, a total nightmare for a young, inexperienced business person like me. One day they would drop off an alcoholic in the crowded cell who might rave drunkenly for a few hours before crashing on the side of the cell. Other times they would haul in a drug dealer. Some of these guys were quite physical and mean to their fellow inmates. Others just sat in a corner and sneered until they got out. A few people had been arrested for murder. I tried to keep away from anyone who looked crazy, mean or murderous, but how far away can you get from anyone when you are confined to a hell hole like that.

Anyone who got caught came first into this little clearing house and then was sent out to another institution suitable to his level of criminality. It wasn't surprising with so many people flowing in and out of the cell that I would run into a few particularly annoying bad apples. Once someone tried to mess with me or my lunch got a very fast lesson.

I jumped him before he could take a bite of my sandwich. He didn't back off and there we were, carrying on all over the cell floor. Those situations ended quite quickly in my favor and helped my fellow cellmates realize that it was not to their advantage to cross the line with me. Until a new troublemaker was put in the cell, everyone decided it was best to leave me alone.

The worst part of this experience for me was not the criminals, the drunks, or the skirmishes, it was the toilet. It was humiliating to go to the bathroom there. There was no wall coverage and anyone who had nothing else to do could stare at you every time you had to relieve yourself. It was disgusting.

After a week in jail, I was let out of the steamy, smelly little cell and brought in for interrogation.

The first interrogation started out on a friendly note. The police officer quite congenially told me that he wanted to help me and he would, anyway he could, if I would just tell him the truth.

I said, "Look, I have nothing to hide. Ask any questions you want."

"One second," he said. He left for a few minutes and brought me a glass of water and some coffee.

I eagerly drank up the coffee, practically in a gulp. He smiled in a most friendly way.

"Hans," he said, "we all know what you do for a living. And we definitely know that you are not a hardened criminal, like some of the types you may have run across in our little cell."

"Thank you," I said. "Finally ..."

"But," he interrupted, "we do know, for sure, that you knew the parts were stolen."

I shook my head.

"Look," he smiled again, "all you need to do is to give us a couple of names and I'll help you get out of that poisonous little hell hole."

"I'd love to give you some names," I said, looking him in the eyes and not seeing exactly what I was hoping for.

"If you don't tell us—confess to—what we already know, you may wind up staying here a long time."

"You know something, sir," I said, finding that unfortunate coldness in his stare, despite the persistent smile, "I'd be glad to confess to you if I was guilty because I truly hate this place, and making a deal with you would be a perfect solution."

He stared at me, patient, waiting ...

"But, unfortunately, I am as much a victim as the guys who own the warehouse that got pilfered. I would love to see you nab the thieves. I'm not one of them, and I did not know the parts were stolen property either. So ... there cannot be any evidence against me. You know, you should really let me go."

I then smiled at him in a very kindly manner and waited for his answer.

He sighed and looked at me, then left the room. I neatly placed the cup back on its saucer and got ready to go back to my cell. He got the message, I said to myself.

Two minutes later another officer came in. He was dressed quite a bit sloppier than the other one. He looked at me for a couple of seconds, and scowled. He then reached out so fast that even I would have a hard time responding if I dared, and grabbed a large chunk of my hair, then slapped me very hard in the face. It was so painful, tears flowed involuntarily from my eyes.

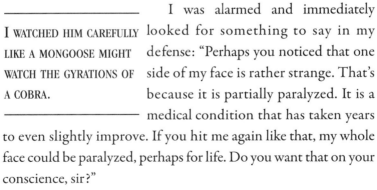

I WATCHED HIM CAREFULLY LIKE A MONGOOSE MIGHT WATCH THE GYRATIONS OF A COBRA.

I was alarmed and immediately looked for something to say in my defense: "Perhaps you noticed that one side of my face is rather strange. That's because it is partially paralyzed. It is a medical condition that has taken years to even slightly improve. If you hit me again like that, my whole face could be paralyzed, perhaps for life. Do you want that on your conscience, sir?"

There was no blood. Aside from the momentary redness, there was probably no visible effect from the blow. The new guy, who I believe now was part of a staged good cop-bad cop scenario, stopped for a moment, perhaps to weigh some of the personal danger involved to him if he truly hurt me. I didn't get the good cop-bad cop thing. I only knew I was cornered.

In seconds, I fell back on my "attack first" scenario, but dismissed it immediately. I tried to think of another strategy, but clearly I was grasping at straws. Though I wasn't sure of just what to do, I decided in a feint by breathing heavily, as though I might be convulsive, going into some kind of fit.

I didn't believe he would buy it, but it threw him off guard.

I watched him carefully like a mongoose might watch the gyrations of a cobra. I surmised in seconds that his pause was only based on a selfish reflection, and from the slight movement of his hands, I believed he would strike me again, perhaps even harder.

His right hand was trembling, perhaps with the anticipation of the blow he would deal to this non-repentant spark plug bandit, when I noticed it stopped. In micro-seconds, I surmised he was about to strike and I jumped up suddenly, instinctively, managing to get to a window faster than he could get to me.

Once there, I hit my head into the glass so hard that the window broke. He was startled by my explosive act of self-destruction.

I couldn't see much, because blood was running down my face and had clouded my eyes, but I could see that he was worried that, indeed, I might be insane.

Again, for a moment, he was too startled to do anything, except to creep toward me, cautiously, but still ready to do something. I quickly put my head through the broken window. If he grabbed me in the wrong way, he could cut me badly, maybe cut an artery in my neck.

So I paused there while he thought about his next assault. I then said quietly, "Look, asshole, if you try to touch me again, or even come closer, I will lift my head up and down and what you see will be much worse, the stuff of major bleeding and major scaring. And, you fuck, you had better kill me now, because, if I do this and stay alive, I'm going to tell everyone that you did this to me. And you will be thrown into the fucking jail instead of me."

Now he appeared genuinely puzzled. I managed to ward off his attack by attacking myself first. I did throw the bastard off, even though an attack against him would be the thing he most desired. Then he could rip me to pieces.

"When you take me out of here, no one will believe that it wasn't you, you fucking coward. And I hope you go to hell, along with that other son of a bitch."

I turned slightly.

The guy was now lost in his thoughts, uncertain of how to deal with the problem, now beyond his control.

"Go ahead, you bastard, make your move. I don't give a goddamn what happens to me anymore."

He stared at me and the broken window helplessly.

"Calm down," he said finally.

He then moved to tap me lightly on the shoulder, something he probably thought would be a comforting gesture, but then quickly withdrew his hand. His fear had hooked him. He still wanted his job.

It wasn't too long before Mr. Good Cop, now Mr. Nice Guy, came back.

Mr. Nice Guy profusely apologized and gave me a towel so I could clean myself up. The result was that all the visible damage amounted to was a few little scratches from my window tantrum. In terms of the metaphors I love that are drawn from professional fighting, Mr. Nice Guy was the "good side" of the tag team, whose job was to break down the resistance of bad guys.

So, when Mr. Nice Guy brought me back to my cell, no one bothered me anymore.

After three weeks, I was released because there was no evidence that I had stolen anything.

Oh, yes, I was lucky, but I was also disillusioned. What happened to me was not right. It was not based on trying to find out who was guilty and who was innocent. It was based on specific individuals trying to get brownie points for a capture, arrest and indictment, no matter who was guilty. If I had not been clever and lucky, I would not have eased over toward that window and found a way to scare the shit out of the good cop-bad cop tag team.

I became very curious about our justice system.

CHAPTER

8

# Finally Out ... and an Offer

*Despite myself, I felt my optimism creeping back.*

When I got out of jail, Tony Zach picked me up with Herta, my girlfriend. She was excited and kissed and hugged me 100 times. Tony embraced me warmly, saying, "Come on, man, cheer up! You're finally out of that cesspool. I'll bet you'd like to have some real food."

I smiled grimly, since, believe it or not, my jaw still ached from the Bad Cop's slap three weeks prior. I think he may have loosened some teeth. But, probably, it was a sense of hopelessness I had, that somehow life was unjust and I wasn't really protected anymore. It was a spiritual thing, like tiny, painful gossamers of fear had been let out of a Pandora's box in the corner of my mind.

"You're worried about money, aren't you, Hansi?"

I wasn't thinking about it at the moment, but when he said that, a few

------

"I THINK YOU NEED A TUX AND A FEW MARTINIS BEFORE YOUR AUDITION."

------

more gossamers floated out of my unconscious, and life as a butcher didn't look that appealing without my highly successful, but now defunct, moonlighting operation.

So I replied affirmatively.

"I think I'm sick of cutting up meat and bossing around people who cut it up, too. Maybe I should move to Hollywood. I think they're looking for the new James Bond."

Tony looked at me in the rags I managed to salvage from the prison, and the bags underneath my eyes and my slumping, depressed shoulders.

"I think you need a tux and a few martinis before your audition."

"I don't like martinis," I said. "I like manhattans, though. You could fix me up with a few of those."

He then slapped me on my back. "Okay, you got a deal. Hey, I'll take you to the restaurant Steirer Eck. That should cheer you up." The Steirer Eck was a very exquisite and expensive restaurant.

But since I still looked depressed, he came closer and whispered to me, "I think I better cheer you up before I waste good money on a great dinner that you probably won't even enjoy."

"Oh, you got connections in Hollywood now, Tony?"

"Nope, but I do have a place for you with me, in my business. It ain't Hollywood, but it will sure make you better money than you make now. And you won't have to steal any spark plugs to get by."

He looked to see if I even slightly smiled at his friendly little jibe.

I just couldn't lighten up, but I did nod my head affirmatively. "Shit, I thought you had Hollywood connections."

Still, even though I couldn't bring myself to feel any enthusiasm at the moment, his offer started to grow on me from that moment.

After all, I did admire the guy. Did he not drive a silver-gray Mercedes 280 SEL convertible, with a sleek, dark blue roof and leather seats designed in the same color as the roof while I drove a Mini Cooper? Don't get me wrong, this was my first car and I loved it, but it was for sure not a Mercedes. Tony was always throwing money around and always had a beautiful girl fawning all over him. Although I'd never admit it to him, he was actually a role model for me.

Maybe he was offering me a real chance. God knows I needed it. Because, despite the occasional flash of glamour of the disco, and the neat little moonlighting bonuses, my life was filled with drudgery. For most of my life, I had been in wage slave prison, and I didn't like it.

But, if my income was raised substantially, and I was given more freedom and a moment to enjoy my life, maybe there was some hope for me.

The more I thought about working with Tony, the more I liked it.

The fact was, I hated living in the cruddy, old high rise in that tiny, microscopic apartment in Vienna. If I worked for Tony, I could still live in the apartment in my parents' restaurant.

If I went back home, I would not have to pay rent and Tony's business was in Ebenfurth, eight miles away from the restaurant, two miles closer to where Herta was living. My job and my girlfriend were now practically at my doorstep and things started to take on a rosy hue. Despite myself, I felt my optimism creeping back.

CHAPTER

9

# Change—The Auto Business

*My job evolved and it became far more than selling cars.*

A few days after I got out of jail, I decided to talk to Tony Zach about his offer. So I made it over to his tire store at a busy little corner in Ebefurth, just a hop and a jump from Wiener Neustadt. I had been there before and had managed to sell him a few premium auto parts.

He seemed happy to see me, and we chatted about a new business he wanted to start.

His idea, in a nutshell, was to import small trucks from Germany, most of them Mercedes trucks with different chassis, including those equipped for specialized types of hauling: refrigerated vehicles, flatbeds, box dare, platform tipper, suitcase dare, removal vans, and box vans that you could build out inside to make an RV.

All these vehicles, when new, were very expensive. There would be a big demand for these types of used vehicles in Austria.

In order to get these types of cars, he had connected with a guy named Walter Pincolits, who initially presented him with the idea for this type of import business.

Walter claimed to know exactly where we could find these vehicles in Germany. In our proposed business roles, Walter would be the locator of this profitable inventory and I would be the key salesman, also in charge of getting them ready to be presented to customers.

Tony offered me a monthly $2,000 salary to start. In addition to this quite reasonable monthly stipend, I would get a $100 for every car we sold, whether or not I was directly responsible for the sale. This would be delivered to me, along with the monthly salary, at the end of the month.

That deal sounded pretty good to a nineteen year old living in Austria in 1973. The average monthly salary at that time for the average worker was between $800 and $1,200. I agreed in a heartbeat.

One week later, Walter and I were off to Munich and Stuttgart to buy the first vehicles.

Once there, Walter introduced me to dealers in a wide range of locations in various towns in and near those cities. Some of these dealers had a remarkably large stock to draw from. We wound up buying ten vehicles.

Walter received a commission of $200 for every vehicle we bought.

Once the vehicles were purchased, I was in charge of getting them to Austria. During that time, there was nothing like a united Europe. In Austria in particular, Mercedes vehicles were much more expensive than in Germany. Plus, you had to deal with customs, transporting the vehicles and finally restoring them. After all that work, you then had to get a government inspection and a new title. Believe me, the last part was the toughest.

Back in Austria, I had the cars undercoated and sealed. Then we spray-painted and fixed them up, at which time they really looked like new. The great part of this business was, despite all the work, we bought a vehicle for $2,000 or $3,000, fixed it up and invested maybe $1,000 to $2,000 and then sold it for $10,000 to $12,000.

Wow! We were making around $5,000 to $6,000 of pure profit per car, sometimes doubling or tripling our investment. We started slowly. In the first couple of months, we sold maybe four or five cars. But in a short time, we sold between ten and fifteen cars a month. It seemed like we had stumbled on something serious.

I worked very hard, probably more than seventy hours a week, but the money was very, very good.

We got a lot of our business by placing ads in the newspaper. When someone called us, I developed a unique way of responding, somewhat different than the tactics of an ordinary car salesman, who would try and set up an appointment at their own facility.

Many times, I found that people who called in often found it inconvenient to come by. They would say something like, "I am forty miles away, but maybe I can come over next week."

As soon as the client tried to delay my presentation, I immediately offered to drive to his home or business and show him the car.

When I arrived, I did not use any kind of closing technique. I simply showed him how the car was sleek and clean and in perfect mechanical order, as it always was.

This was away from the normally paranoid atmosphere of a typical car dealership with its highly pressured methods of handling customers. I was able to perform quite differently than most car salesmen, achieving an average closing ratio of 80 percent. In terms of the average sales performance, what I was doing was nothing short of amazing. Pretty soon, we were selling around twenty to thirty vehicles a month. Now I was really busy.

One day I showed a 36-foot box truck for furniture delivery. The client was impressed and bought it. I was now on the way back to the shop to adjust a couple of things on the truck specifically for his use. It was already 10 PM and I was about 50 miles from home, when in front of me, there were blinking lights from police cars and the entire street was blocked. Climbing from my truck to see what was going on, a policeman told me that it would be best to turn around. He explained to me how I could go around that area. It was late and I was tired and pissed and asked myself why this was happening to me.

WHEN I PUSHED BACK, I HIT HIM EXACTLY BETWEEN THE TWO SIDE DOORS, IN THE MIDDLE OF HIS CAR AND BENT IT LIKE A U.

I walked to the back of my truck to make sure nobody was standing behind me. I would have to push far back to the left side, to get in position to turn in the other direction. I looked there and no one was parked behind me or on that side either, so I climbed in and pushed back, slowly and carefully.

But there was some kind of resistance. I drove a couple of feet forward and then pushed back a little bit stronger, and again, I could not move back. Perhaps there was a rock on the side of the street blocking my tire. I had to take a look. When I walked to the back of the truck again, I almost had a heart attack. When I was returning to the cab of the truck to back up, after being sure I was clear, exactly at that moment, that stupid constable drove in and parked in the blind corner of my truck. When I pushed back, I hit him exactly between the two side doors, in the middle of his car and bent it like a U. I couldn't believe the windows of both side doors were broken and the windshield was pushed completely from the frame and was laying on the hood. That car was a total wreck—I had destroyed it.

I walked to the intersection where the constable was directing traffic. I guessed that he was the driver of the destroyed car, and was helping his colleague. I approached him, tapped him on the shoulder and said, "I am sorry, sir, but could you take a look at your car." He was not friendly at all and yelled at me, "Are you nuts? Can't you see I'm busy?"

"I can see that, but I hit your car a little bit, and it would be best if you could take a look."

"What do you mean, you hit my car a little bit?" he said. "It better not have one little scratch. I finally got it back yesterday from the body shop. Some idiot hit me in the rear."

All I could think was, *oh shit, this is not good.* However, he walked back with me to his car, and when we turned the corner of my truck and could see his car, the color of his face changed. He took the cap from his head, threw it on the ground and jumped on it, screaming and yelling like Tarzan.

"SIT DOWN ON THE SIDE OF THE ROAD AND DON'T MOVE, OR I WILL SHOOT YOU, YOU FUCKING ASSHOLE."

"Your fucking idiot. You didn't hit my car, you asshole—you destroyed it! Oh my god, I will kill you. I cannot believe it."

If the situation had not been so serious, I thought this would have been a perfect scene for a movie where you would laugh till you would explode. What was unfolding in front of me as the main actor was unreal and bizarre.

He yelled at me, "Sit down on the side of the road and don't move, or I will shoot you, you fucking asshole."

I was really ready to tell him that he was the asshole to park so stupidly behind my truck, but I thought I better be quiet, or I will never be free from this. Instead, I could sit for the next hundred years in jail. He ran to the front to his colleague and told him what had happened, and then the other idiot came and the screaming and yelling started again like a needle stuck in the groove of a vinyl record. The only difference: it was like a choir now, with the two of them creating an echo chamber. The funny part, my truck had barely a scratch.

I had to wait until the entire car accident that caused this in the first place was cleared. Then they took me to their office, and wrote a detailed record of what happened. When I left, it was 3 AM and I still had to drive home. I finally arrived and Herta asked, "My God, what happened?"

I told her a short version of the story and said, "Please call Tony in the morning and tell him I will come in at noon. Tell him I sold the truck. I need to sleep right now."

I went to bed and thought, *Oh my god, what a day. First it was "great"—I made a great deal, and then I fucked up*. But when I closed my eyes and tried to sleep, I started to laugh when I saw the scene replayed in my mind as the constable saw his car and I saw his face ... it was hilarious!

When I got to the office and told Tony the story, we both laughed and made fun of that poor guy. For us it was not a big deal; insurance would take care of it.

Tony said, "You know what? Manfred Goss was here today and brought a truck back to weld the exhaust pipes. He asked me to go out with him tonight. What do you think?

I said, "Why not; it's a deal."

"Then go home, take a rest and we'll meet at your old working place Café ERIKA."

"Okay."

We met each other 8 PM and had fun till 3 AM.

Manfred drank at least 10 beers, Tony, a bottle of vodka, and me, a lot of manhattans. But the next day, everybody was up at 8 AM, ready to work.

I had to travel through Germany, from Munich to Stuttgart and down to Hamburg, to buy vehicles. Most of the time we already had orders from customers. For example, they were for a refrigerated vehicle, or a tipper vehicle and different chassis, so I had to find them, driving hundreds of miles from one dealer to another until I found the right vehicle. Then I had to drive back, many times myself with one vehicle and with 10 or more others driving the cars home to Austria. When there was a flat bed, we put one on the top. We always drove in a convoy, often as many as 20 cars—one after another.

At home, I was in charge of fixing up the vehicles.

Most of the time I would pick up the parts I needed from Rothmund, a company located in Vienna. The parts I needed most were exhaust system components, commonly broken on used vehicles. The sales manager at Rothmund was Karl Andritz, an awesome guy. From the first moment I met him in the shop, I liked him.

Karl was 6'2", charming and friendly, a real lady's man. No matter what I needed or how difficult a part was to find, Karl was always smiling, helpful and ready to solve my problem.

If he could not find the part at his company, he would try to find it somewhere else, personally ordering it for me and having dropped it off at his company to save me an extra trip. Karl was customer service personified, a very rare person to find, even in those days.

Having connected in this way and enjoying each other's company, we got in the habit of having lunch together. Generally, we went to a restaurant called Styria's Corner, an upper class dining restaurant while his coworkers prepared my parts order. After lunch, I would get the parts and drive them back home. During my frequent visits to Vienna, Karl and I became close friends.

Back in the shop I used to frequently visit Manfred, who worked about a mile away from Tony's tire shop at an engineering company, run by the brothers Peter and Manfred Goss. Of the two, Peter was the oldest by two years. I often went bar hopping with Manfred and Tony, as we had just a couple of days before.

HERTA WAS NEVER HAPPY WHEN MANFRED AND I WENT OUT TOGETHER.

Like Tony, Manfred was ten years older than me. He was a family man with two daughters, but with special rules. There were no comments from Renate, his wife, about his nightlife.

Manfred was quite a character. One of his eccentricities was that he would often spend the entire night on the road. During these frequent excursions, he would come home around 6 AM, but by 8 AM on the dot, he opened up his shop. I never could understand how his wife could put up with him.

The factory was situated in a nicely fenced property, with ten acres of land which was beautifully landscaped. Both brothers lived with their families, each in their own house on that property, close to their father's large, 4,000 square foot house. Their dad was a doctor with his own highly successful practice and was pretty wealthy. He bought this property for his sons, so they both had a secure income and their own business. Both were intelligent, but both dropped out of the university and did not complete their education.

Even though Manfred had his own tool-making engineering company, he took extra time to use his superb precision welding equipment to help me repair certain vehicles or to help create special parts. His brother, Peter, was an arrogant asshole, but I had a lot of fun with Manfred and we became fast friends.

Going barhopping with Manfred was an unbelievable experience. By the time I got home, I was pretty "filled up" and it was always past sunrise. My fiancée Herta was never happy when Manfred and I went out together.

My job evolved and it became far more than selling cars, i.e., transporting the vehicles from Germany to Austria, finding parts for them and dealing with a lot of minutiae for the business. Tony had to sell a lot of vehicles by himself. But, despite that, the business was great and, because of our arrangement, I earned between $4,000 and $6,000 a month. Not bad for someone who was 19 years of age in 1973.

# 10

# My Future ... on a Silver Platter

*I knew it would be risky, even dangerous. I knew
I would be stigmatized forever as that strange,
unpredictable animal—an entrepreneur!
I wanted The Thrill of the Ride!*

Not long after I began working for Tony, a bank offered my parents $250,000 for our restaurant. That was a lot of money in the seventies.

When Franz and I heard about the prospective sale, we weren't all that concerned about it. Franz thought it was too much work to run it. He had begun to work at his certification to become a vocational teacher in a culinary school for cooks and waiters. We were both completely different in what we wanted from life. Franz wanted a sure, steady job, a thought that appalled my entrepreneurial spirit.

Since we were kids, we were completely different. Franz's friends were braggarts and for me, my brother was a strange guy too. Whatever I told him, he knew better. Often our conversations ended in a fight. But even though he was one head taller than me, he could not win. I never quit when we had fights. And even if my nose started to bleed, instead of giving up, it was only an incentive for me to fight harder till he quit. The older we got, the more distance there was between us. I really didn't know what our issue was. It wasn't I didn't love him, for God sakes, he was my brother. I did love him in my special way. But it was really very complicated for me, to understand how he was thinking and what was on his mind. Our point of view about life, business and family was totally different and I still agree with a sentence that I heard from a teacher who said, "It's nothing out there with what is wrong and what is right, it's the point of view, how you see it."

But neither of us ever figured out how to adjust our vision, so at least we could talk in a friendly kind of manner, instead we both took a position to defend ourselves and our opinion. So it ended up with a no way—come along position!

For me life was a challenge, an adventure and fun. I really enjoyed every aspect from it.

I never figured out what my brother really enjoyed, and along our way I quit thinking about it.

So when our parents asked my brother and me what they should do, we both said, "Sell it."

Happy to comply with our wishes, my parents sold the restaurant to the bank for $250,000. Then they bought a two-story house, designed for two families with an identical room layout downstairs and upstairs. I lived downstairs and my brother lived upstairs.

The plan was still that I would eventually receive and take over the restaurant and the butcher shop where my grandparents lived. And my brother would eventually receive the new house that we were both currently living in.

Following the sale, my parents moved to Oslip and refurbished that restaurant and began to run it themselves. For the time being, they closed the butcher shop and thought they would open it when I was ready to take it over.

Herta and I were still together. We were in love and the path to matrimony seemed inevitable.

Accordingly, we bought a property behind her parents' house. Her parents generously gave us half the money to buy that piece of land—around a half an acre.

We wanted to build the house ourselves.

In Austria, when you build a house, you build it for the next 1,000 years, not for the next fifty years, like in America.

To affect this, most Austrian houses are built with bricks and everybody in the family helps out. If one were to hire a construction company, it would be much more expensive and the ordinary family in Austria could not afford it. Because of my busy schedule during the week, I had to work on the house on the weekend. My prospective father-in-law and Herta's grandfather worked with me.

The house was constructed brick by brick. Working on the house was a tough job but, on the other hand, it was unbelievable how much pleasure it was to see it developing.

Herta and I did not have much time together. Our main pleasure was to go out on Friday evening to a nice restaurant and have dinner together. After that, we would go home to the house my parents bought for me and my brother, and enjoy each other's company on weekend evenings, but the entire Saturday and Sunday we were working on our house to build it stone by stone, brick by brick.

We were happy and in love, working on our future together and dreaming of how beautiful it would be. It looked as though, by the time our new house was finished, Herta would complete her education.

And that's the way it happened. By the time I was twenty-one and she was nineteen, she had her certificate and became a teacher in a primary school. At that point, she was making $1,200 a month. A couple of months later, we "officially" got engaged.

I also bought myself a used Mercedes 350 SLC to use on my trips to Germany. As I remember, it was light blue metallic with dark blue leather seats. Gorgeous! My first Mercedes! Everybody in our neighborhood was envious. A kid with a Mercedes 350 SLC was rare in those days.

The Mercedes was my only luxury. Back then, we were saving every dime we had to build our house. The only vacation we took was in the summertime when we spent two weeks in Italy on the beach during Herta's spring break in July and August.

I had been working with Tony for about two years and was making at least $5,000 or more every month. We had grown considerably since we started and had built a 20,000 square foot paint and body shop. One day he called me into his office.

"Look, Hans, I have to talk to you," he said.

"I'm right here," I said. "What's going on?"

"You make really good money with me. I like that. I want you to make money. But, still, things are different now and they need to be fairer. I'm selling more vehicles than you are and we need to make an adjustment. I am willing to pay you $150 instead $100 when you sell a vehicle, but I don't want to pay you a commission on my personal sales."

At first, I was speechless. Then I said, "Now look, Tony, it's not like I just do sales for you. I take care of all these goddamn cars. I help find them; I fix them. I go back and forth between here and Germany for you. Whereas you sit in the office and have total access to anyone who calls in."

> I WAS PISSED, REALLY PISSED. NOW, IT'S NOT GOOD FOR MYSELF OR ANYONE ELSE WHEN I GET THAT FEELING.

He sat there, just quietly looking at me. I was getting more and more angry at this point, but I didn't want to appear too aggressive. "We built up this company together," I calmly said. "We started from scratch. Besides that, we're supposed to be friends."

As I said that, I recalled all the times we went out together, barhopping, often until 3 in the morning. I always thought we were the best friends in the world, sharing our lives with each other. Now this shit. I was shocked.

Tony tried to explain his side. "Look, Hans, step into my shoes for a minute. I was the one who invested my money, including my personal profit, into this property. I built a body shop and a paint-spraying station, totally at my expense. I did not ask you to risk any money like I did."

I was pissed, really pissed. Now, it's not good for myself or anyone else when I get that feeling.

I understood that Tony had taken a risk. On the other hand, it was not as though all I did was sell cars or that I was getting the same level of reward as he was. Every car that was sold had my imprint on it. I either had picked it up, ordered parts for it, supervised the repair and bodywork, or sold it myself. When I had an impending sale, I might drive forty or eighty miles at my own risk to make the sale.

I was an unappreciated asset that had helped build the business.

Trying to be careful with my temper, I said, "Okay, we'll try it for one or two months, but if it doesn't work for me, then 'sayonara.' I will find my own way."

> FINALLY, IT BECAME CLEAR AS GLASS. I SAW A GOLDEN OPPORTUNITY IN THE MIDST OF THE RANDOM, BATTERED RAMBLINGS OF MY MIND.

I left the office and went back to work, but, for me, the story was already over. I could not believe how much of a moron he was. I thought, *What a greedy bastard!*

I was working a minimum of twelve hours a day, sometimes driving back and forth between Austria and Germany in one day—16 hours with no rest. Often, I drove long into the night, and now this bullshit! Tony made a profit of at least $80,000 to $120,000 monthly. For sure, he invested in his offices, buildings and more, but they still belonged to him. In fact, everything belonged to him and nothing to me.

I had helped him build his company from scratch, and that company was really growing. I was his best worker and managed the entire import business and, in my eyes, I was some kind of a partner with him as we had started this business from scratch together.

I could not get over it. It wasn't just unfairness about money. The money was replaceable. It was a personal thing. What should I do? I was being eaten alive by uncertainty, uncertainty about who I could trust, uncertainty about losing a friend, and how to handle the situation.

I was so troubled about Tony's offer and the thinking behind it, I saw my work ethic begin to dramatically slide. For a couple of days, I could not sleep. I was nervous as hell and my mind was racing. I felt I had to make a decision. Should I stay a minute more under these conditions? If I left, now or later, what should I do?

Herta asked me a couple of times what was going on, but I told her nothing. I didn't want to make her nervous and scared about the future.

Finally, it became clear as glass. I saw a golden opportunity in the midst of the random, battered ramblings of my mind. Tony, who looked, unfortunately, like he soon would be my former friend, had handed me the brass ring on the carousel.

He had given me the ticket that I had always wanted, but had never dared to ask.

You see, at that magic moment, I assessed my chances at personal survival, not by stopping what I was doing and seeking another fluffy job, but going out on my own, staying exactly where I was comfortable. For the moment, it was buying and selling imported cars!

And why not?

Tony and his associate, Walter, had taught me where I could get the vehicles. I knew how to fix them up, and I knew how to use them to turn a high profit, yet give people the car of their dreams. All I really had to do was to find a perfect property for my own car business, and I would be in business by myself.

At that time, I swore to myself I would never work for somebody else again.

I knew it would be risky, even dangerous. I knew I would be stigmatized forever as that strange, unpredictable animal—an entrepreneur! I knew there would be ups and downs—maybe not in the exact way they would happen later—but I wanted the risk. Yes, I wanted the risk and I wanted the wealth. And, above all, having felt cloistered and subdued by circumstance my whole life, I wanted the "thrill of the ride."

I thought about my own family. My grandpa and his father—my parents too—all that we were ... We were entrepreneurs. four generations, possibly more, I really didn't know.

I had made a promise to myself, a promise I have always kept ... even up to today.

### *I would never, I mean never in my life work for somebody else again.*

That one flashing revelation of the value of that ticket to freedom that Tony had handed me on a silver platter was the courage to be myself.

I looked back on my decision in my dream and I had to smile. For forty-two years now, I had never broken the covenant I made with myself. Already, at 21, I had been an independent entrepreneur. Hallelujah. What a ride. Now, I am on my way again with nothing, and into a totally new world thousands of miles away.

I recognized entrepreneurs are not just in it for the success or the profit. I think they are in it because they live for the highs and lows ... and they know that no matter what comes their way, it is they alone who make it or break it. Entrepreneurs depend on no one but themselves to define their success, and allow no one but themselves to use the word *failure*. They may fall, but they fall forward. They are the risk takers. The creative disruptors who don't just break the rules, they throw away the game, choosing to forge their own path, answering only to themselves.

This is a unique group, filled with men such as college dropouts Bill Gates, Steve Jobs and Mark Zuckerman who put their mark on technology and women like fashion visionary Sara Blakey, media mogul Oprah Winfrey, and author turned entrepreneur J.K. Rowling. Many in this class opt out of degrees, titles and accolades, instead, working far too hard on their own education—in the school of hard knocks.

This is the life of the entrepreneur. It starts with one simple idea. It starts with the realization and loud declaration, somewhere in the person's life, that he or she will never, ever work for anyone else again. That is how my real story began.

So welcome to the thrill of my ride!

# 11

# Dream Break

*I organized my mind and quickly remembered
where I stopped.*

I woke up again, took my eye mask down, and sighed deeply. The lady next to me looked at me strangely, so I looked straight into her eyes. Immediately she looked away, and I understood her entire person in an instant. She was perhaps in her forties, pretty, shoulder-length brunette hair, and very elegant.

My brief view showed me big brown eyes, a little bit of an exotic face with perfectly formed lips. Nice boobs that I could see—her blouse had a very low neckline.

Classy designer clothes—could be Chanel, or a fancy Italian designer.

My judgment: classy, extravagant and high maintenance. Maybe she was pretty nice, or she could possibly be an arrogant rich bitch! However, I was being careful with my opinion; I had learned I was not always right.

I LOOKED AT MY WATCH. IT WAS STILL MY GOLDEN ROLEX.

It was odd though, how quickly I understood every detail about that lady—how I put everything about her together. She fit perfectly into the world that I was leaving. I had not forgotten how quickly I assess information about somebody—almost in a heartbeat.

I guess I learned that skill over the years, and it was still working, even in my present, screwed up situation.

Could Monte Carlo, the playground of the rich and famous, be her backdrop? My first take told me it could be. I wondered what story she had to tell. She did not look happy at all. I also imagine sitting next to me was, for her, not exciting in the least. I had on an ordinary shirt, but at least I wore my Armani jeans. I had only three pair of jeans, a couple of shirts and two pair of shoes in my luggage. For sure, I could not compare myself to her, and it was not in my thoughts to do so.

I looked at my watch. At least, it was still my golden Rolex, showing me only three hours had passed since we left Monaco with nine hours more to go. Now, I really had to smile. I did not forget my only valuable possession from my rich days—my cherished Rolex. I thought with amusement that it should be a ticket to her world ... but I had to use the restroom and I had the window seat. I had no choice but to ask the lady to let me out.

She looked at me and said with an Italian accent, "Sure, sir." It seemed she was not so snappish after all.

I made my way to the restroom, which was occupied so I started to make small talk with the nice stewardess. She spoke fluent German and that made my day.

On my way back, I ordered another whisky and then slipped into my seat.

The stewardess brought me my drink, smiled and spoke in a really friendly manner. I saw from the corner of my eye, the conversation got the attention of my neighbor, but right now, I didn't care. I really needed to get back to my past.

I took up my eye mask, looked provokingly to the lady at my side and said, "See you later." She only rolled her eyes and made a sound like "phh" and that was that.

I organized my mind and quickly remembered where I had stopped.

# 12

# The Chance and the Breakaway

*Speak of entrepreneurial ecstasy! I was only
20 years old and I owned my own business.*

I had to find a property immediately before I ran out of cash.

Knowing the area where I was living well was a plus for me. Traveling to Vienna frequently, my idea was to get a property on a highway that would take me there in the most direct way.

It had to be one of the main roads with a lot of traffic. In terms of location, I think—no I knew—it would be a very big improvement over Tony's location. And in dealing with the used car import business, location was a factor that could be critical to growth.

I found 10 acres at an intersection on a main road to Vienna— a small village near the highway. It was 10 miles away from the city where I was born. It was the perfect location.

The funny part, it was close to my friend, Hans Holz, who managed his parents' Airplane Bar. The bar was attached to a building housing Kegel lanes, the Austrian form of bowling. Proceeding toward Vienna, and coming to the end of that little town, you would find my car lot on the left side of the highway.

This property belonged to a very old Jewish guy, and I made an appointment with him. At the appointment, I convinced him of the value of the enterprise I was going to create on his lot, and he sold me the lot, financing our arrangement himself.

It was a high risk for me. It was an exceedingly tough contract. I had to make regular payments or I would definitely lose the property. But despite the conditions, there was no real question for me—this was perfect! But I would need some help. No bank was about to give me the $300,000 I needed to buy this piece of land. The help I needed was to come from the current owner ... what I needed was owner financing to buy the building.

And I got it.

After I had the contract in my hands, I immediately went to Tony and told him I was quitting.

He was shocked and tried to turn me around. He even tried to tempt me by offering to return to our original agreement, where I would get $100 for every car. Perhaps a few days ago I would have done it, but now it was too late.

After I refused, he asked me what I was going to do and, frankly, I lied to him. I told him that first I would take a vacation for a couple of weeks and then I would work for a couple of weeks on my house to try and accelerate our progress. Only after that would I make a decision.

He then offered me a part-time position. I declined, saying that I needed a break. After that, I would stop and assess what was going on.

Nothing could have been further from the truth.

Actually, I did the opposite, diving completely into my new business. I worked like crazy, building a fence with Herta's grandfather and purchasing a portable office building, similar to those used on construction sites. After two weeks, I had a fenced area and an office. And, I had $80,000 in cash saved. This became my startup capital.

Then my friend, Helmut Schaerf, and I started talking about building a business together. My goal was to create a business with Helmut before I left Tony, but it had no chance to succeed, at least then. What happened was that the women got in the way! It turned out that our wives sabotaged our working together by their hatred for each other. I knew one thing for sure, when you start with trouble, it would end with trouble.

I liked that guy ... he was kind of unbelievable with his skills and really multi-talented. And, he was also a cousin to the Schaerf Coffee Machine empire. Helmut was a chef who created delicious meals. And he also was a mechanic; he could fix freaking everything. To me, it would have been an ideal fit for where I saw my new direction.

Helmut introduced me to Vick Mair—a talented mechanic who had been working with him on the side for years. Vick had a master's degree and worked at a dealership for BMW close by. He was three years older than I was, and an awesome guy. Vick had golden hands and could fix practically anything. Of course, I wanted him and offered him $2,500 a month, which was a generous offer for a mechanic at the time. He agreed and soon I was off to Germany to begin building my inventory.

My first purchases were made at all the places I knew well from my work with Tony. After Vick and I fixed them up, I sold my first vehicles on my own lot on March 23, 1974. From that first sale until the end of April, I sold eight vehicles and made $24,000 profit. I couldn't believe it! I was in German car import heaven!

Speak of entrepreneurial ecstasy! I was only 21 years old and I owned my own business.

Tony was furious when he discovered that I was his competition, calling and screaming at me, "You're an asshole and have betrayed me."

"Bullshit, Tony—what would you have done if you had been in my shoes?" In a way, I tried to be conciliatory, in the sense that I wanted him to see that it wasn't an act of malice, but an act of survival, using whatever resources I had acquired to stay alive.

But this logic-reasoning route failed completely, and Tony ended our relationship on a really rough note. I was sad. The fact was that I really liked Tony. To now know that we would be enemies for the rest of our lives gave me no joy whatsoever.

As my business grew, I built an 8,000 square foot shop where we could fix the vehicles and a two-story office building. With its growth, I could demonstrate revenues and a profit and banks would talk to me—I got my first $200,000 loan from one. During this time, I sold a lot of Mercedes concrete and dump trucks to Lebanon.

Why Lebanon?

Back in 1974, Lebanon was known as the "Switzerland of the East." Today it doesn't have that reputation, but then, it enjoyed a period of relative calm and prosperity, driven by tourism, agriculture and banking.

Lebanon attracted large numbers of tourists, such that the capital, Beirut, was referred to as the "Paris of the Middle East." During that time, the construction business was booming and guys from Lebanon were coming to Austria looking for used trucks. Their favorite was the Mercedes truck with the hood in front.

When the Lebanese came knocking on my door, I found the vehicles they were looking for, but, after a time, it got more and more difficult to get them. I wasn't alone in my efforts because these young men were banging on every Austrian dealer's door. But I was tenacious—I scoured Germany for the trucks and was averaging around $10,000 profit per vehicle and selling four to five of them every month.

At the end of 1975, I had hired 20 employees and consistently held 40 to 50 vehicles in stock. Yes, the truck business was doing well.

In addition to our specialty in sales, we offered services on all kinds of vehicles. I added dedicated areas for repair and service as well as a body shop with a special enclosure for paint-spraying.

After Vick was my manager for a while, I put him in charge of all repair jobs and gave him a very generous raise. Vick never failed me once. He was hard working and loyal to a fault, a true friend as well as an employee. Without question, he worked as hard for me as he would have worked for his own business, never complaining, but doing each job meticulously.

There were ten acres of land in the back of my property that I converted to a junkyard, a great help to my business. In it, we stored vehicles we couldn't fix completely and trade-ins that we still needed to work on. When we needed parts, we first determined if we could take them from a vehicle in our junkyard. If we could, we would save a lot of money instead of purchasing parts from others. As a new side business, a lot of people came by looking for used parts—my "junkyard" became the go-to resource—and a nice little profit center was developed there, too.

AT THE END OF 1975, I HAD ACQUIRED 20 EMPLOYEES AND CONSISTENTLY HELD 40 TO 50 VEHICLES IN STOCK.

In 1975, the Lebanese civil war broke out and turned the "Paris of the Middle East" into a war-ravaged nightmare of broken bodies and buildings. And, I lost a very important and profitable part of my business.

Owing to the demand for the Mercedes trucks and other favored items sought by the Lebanese buyers, I had intentionally accumulated as large an inventory as I could afford. These vehicles had been hard to find, so I horded them and kept them at a relatively high price when there was a demand for them.

As the civil war commenced, demand for these vehicles dwindled to almost nothing because our local buyers did not like our Lebanese clients' favorite brands of cars.

Yet, the investment I had put out every year was substantial and by the time of the Lebanese war, I had about 70 to 80 vehicles in stock.

# Harry to the Rescue

A lot of parts got stolen from the junkyard. My solution was to buy two little German Shepherd puppies to train as guard dogs.

When I think about it today, buying these dogs was kind of stupid. Puppies need time to grow up. Their usefulness, for the moment, was confined to some of my clients picking them up for a minute or two and petting them and maybe relaxing a bit more as we launched into a discussion about their prospective purchase.

Then one day, the inevitable happened. Someone stole the puppies. Now both my parts *and* my dogs were being stolen.

This got me really mad, and I called a friend of mine who raised Rottweilers. I went over to his kennel. He had only one Rottweiler available at the moment. I didn't need puppies ... I needed a *real* dog.

When I went over to see the dog, he was jumping around like a deranged kangaroo and barking like crazy.

"What the hell is going on with this dog?" I asked.

"He has some hair growing on his eyeball. It is very painful every time he blinks. So he barks and goes nuts every few minutes. He desperately needs an operation but I can't put out the money right now."

This immense animal was a 90 pound Rottweiler—a huge, angry, slobbering nightmare of a dog.

"Look," my friend said, "despite everything, this guy is a pure breed, but an enormous problem for me. Even in his cage, people are scared of him. I'll give him to you for free, but you'll have to fix his eye or he'll be a useless, barking maniac."

"Holy shit," I said. "That dog is a monster, but I'll take him. What's his name?"

"Harry," my friend said.

I looked at the dog and said, "Okay, Harry, you're acting like you are insane, but maybe there's something I can do with you and you can do for me."

I had come in a truck that had only one seat row so Harry had to sit next to me. Every time I changed gears, he hit his nose against the dashboard, not hard mind you, but enough to blame me for it. It compelled him to curl his lips revealing his massive, pointed teeth—all the while looking very pissed off and growling somewhere deep in his throat. It was a peculiarly ugly, menacing tone and I would lie if I said I was not fucking scared. Finally, I got him to the office, my throat and limbs still intact. I left him there to cool off for the rest of the day and I was happily surprised when nothing happened.

FROM THAT DAY ON, HE WAS MY BEST FRIEND.

The next day I took him to a vet and paid $500 for Harry's eye surgery. As I gave the money to the receptionist, I wondered if his ordeal might make him even meaner.

But when I came to pick him up, Harry seemed quite different. First, he looked at me and then pushed against my leg with his big old head. Was this a sign of affection? I was now skeptical, thinking back a few days ago when I thought he was going to eat me alive.

Suddenly, he jumped up on me, his front paws resting on my shoulders. A cold chill came over me and I was ready to shit in my pants. I glanced into his eyes, perhaps the last clear thing I would see before I was torn to little pieces by this insane dog monster.

But as I looked, all I saw was pure love, culminating with a few of the warmest, pleasant doggy face-licks possible on this planet. Slowly, I realized that I had underestimated Harry's intelligence. He knew, somehow—I mean actually knew—that I was the one that rescued him from that incessant pain.

From that day on, he was my best friend. Whenever I was in my office or outside, that dog was with me. And when I took him for his morning walk and stopped to talk to somebody, he always strategically placed himself between me and the other person.

I soon saw that Harry was a natural bodyguard and relentless in his vigilance. If someone touched me—a light pat on the back or just a simple handshake—the person would soon hear a low growl and notice Harry watching him or her like a hawk, reacting ever so slightly to the tiniest movement.

Now feeling that my property was secure, I broke down and bought a jet black German Shepherd puppy. I named him Caesar and he also got big! A year later, he looked like a big black wolf.

The two dogs took good care of my property and seemed to really get along. I now had my guards and it paid off. Nobody stole parts anymore.

## Celebrating Success

Ferrence Barat, my friend from my disc jockey days, came by one day to get his car fixed. He sat around and drank coffee and read the newspaper that was delivered daily. Although his car was in a good state of repair, he returned the next day in time to get some hot coffee and read the newspaper, occasionally chatting with me—between pages and sips. This went on for a good part of the time I ran that business—Ferrence became a fixture of my waiting room. He had a reputation for being rather rich but watching his pennies—and I guess he found a good money saving deal when he first visited my office.

Although I knew him previously, his visits sort of troubled me at first, but then we began to chat more. I had only known him very casually before, but the more we talked, the more I realized how educated and interesting he was.

Ferrence, who was not married, and had no kids, lived the life of a successful bachelor, often accompanied by a pretty girl as a companion, much younger than he was. He seemed so stingy with his money that I found his ability to attract ladies rather unbelievable, but he did attract them.

One day he told me emphatically, "Most people buy things they don't need, with money they don't have, to impress people they don't like."

It is a hard truth to realize but critical if you want to have a decent "geo-positioning system" for navigating in the real world of business.

Our friendship grew and sometimes we brought our ladies to a Heuriger on a weekend or for fun after a hard day's work.

A Heuriger, which is also called a Buschenschank, is a typical Viennese hangout with unique ambiance. A true Heuriger is owned by a winemaker who serves wine from grapes grown on his own soil. Food is generally served as a small buffet and the selection, although relatively small, can be quite good.

Don't confuse it with a fine-dining restaurant—it is not. The décor is ridiculously simple—an interior furnished with simple wooden tables and wooden seats. In most cases, there is an outside place to sit with your friends in a grassy area with beautiful huge, old trees. We enjoyed sitting outside, Ferrence with a different lady almost every time and I with my Herta. I met a lot of new faces, "floating" along on Ferrence's arm, an ever-changing stream of young, charming women.

Heurigens are known for their live music—often quite colorful—and often with two singers: one with an accordion and the other with double-necked guitar. They serenade the customers, table by table, playing traditional songs often by request. The songs are very popular and the audience chimes in. After a few glasses of wine, Ferrence and I had no scruples about joining in, singing together somewhat disharmoniously, perhaps better described as howling like two hungry wolves. We may have sounded ridiculous, but even the patrons around us seemed to like it because we did it with such good will, and it was funny and entertaining.

⁓

Ferrence bought some car repairs from me over the years, but not all that much. In fact, I turned out to be a much better customer of his than he was of mine. Ferrence was into watches and jewelry in a very big-time way.

For instance, I bought my first gold Rolex from him, a hugely valuable status symbol but also one hell of a watch.

I paid $5,000 dollar for it, at that time a lot of money for any kind of a watch. It was a Rolex "Oyster Perpetual Day—Date Model" with a full presidential bracelet in 18 karat gold. I was really proud of it. It was, for me, a personal symbol of my progress and still today I have the same watch and I wear it every single day.

I didn't stop there, though. I bought Herta a Lady Rolex as well as rings, bracelets and diamonds over the years.

At the time we started going out with Ferrence, Herta and I were still unmarried, but it was clear that we would state a definitive date when the house project was finished.

In certain ways, we were certainly a strange couple. I was full of business, spending every day on the road hunting for cars. She was a competent, but still somewhat ordinary Austrian school teacher in an elementary school setting. Unknown to both of us, we were beginning to travel in two entirely different directions.

# Branching Out Again

*The Mercedes dealers hated us passionately and tried
everything they could to stop us, but they couldn't
do anything against us legally.*

I did not talk about my business at home with Herta or her parents. They didn't understand what the hell I was talking about. When I would talk about my dreams and goals, Herta's parents—even my own parents—looked at me like I was crazy.

Both my family and my future in-laws thought I was a megalomaniac. But the more they told me to be careful and not to expand so fast, the more I pressed down on the gas pedal.

On the weekends, we still worked on our house. Every weekend, I would regularly hear them chant, "Oh my God, I hope everything will go well ..." It was as though everything I did was poised on the edge of a growing sinkhole. It wasn't so much their general "well wishes" that got to me, but the "Oh my God ..." prefix and the panic in their voices. Ah, entrepreneurship, we who play the game pay such a high price when we take our hearts and souls into a game that few people ever even wish to play!

Four or five times a week, I would stop off at the Airplane Bar on my way home. It was relaxing to sit down with my friend, Hans Holz, with a cup of espresso and chat about our lives and adventures.

Hans' brother, Siegi, was six years younger than Hans, about 19 at the time and I was 23. He was quite tall, about six feet, two inches, and he played a lot of soccer. Siegi and I, over a period of time, became very good friends. One thing interesting about him was his obsession with coin-operated video games and slot machines.

Siegi's parents had another café in Baden, 20 miles from Wiener Neustadt in the direction of Vienna. He lived in an apartment over that café and basically supervised the ten different video games and slot machines in the business below. His dad split the profits with him, as though he were a vendor.

Despite his age, Siegi enjoyed the fact that I treated him like an adult. He and his brother, Hans, were known as two brothers who would stand by each other, no matter what, quite the opposite of my brother, Franz, and me.

The Holz brothers were known to be wealthy. And, as is sometimes the case, this often led to considerable jealousy among the young blue-collar men who hung around drinking holes in the area. So, it wasn't unusual for the brothers to be provoked into a fight.

The young men who decided to take on the Holz brothers soon learned that they had spent their time unwisely. I never saw or heard of the brothers losing a fight. They were both strong, tough and used to fighting.

I was happy to be on their side, in fact, to be considered part of their family.

Whenever I visited the Airplane Bar, if Siegi was there, he would head toward me immediately, no matter what he was doing. After a while, both of them came regularly to visit me on the car lot.

## My Expansions Begin ...

In 1976, I decided to import used BMWs and Mercedes and to have more variety: expensive sports cars from Germany. During that time, I met Gerhard Hoefler and quickly went into business with him. An unbelievably talented trader and dealer, Gerhard had great contacts with big rent-a-car companies in Germany.

When Mercedes announced a model change, the dealership in Germany got it first. The Austrian Mercedes Dealer got access to the new model some six months later. But that access only meant that the Austrian dealership had the right to introduce the public to the model and take orders. Once placing an order, the poor customers might have to wait from six months to a year to actually get their car. This was a long and painful wait for hungry Mercedes aficionados.

Besides prioritizing German dealerships, the Mercedes company also prioritized all the big German rent-a-car companies. Hertz, for instance, would get the cars much earlier than any Mercedes dealer in Austria. Gerhard saw a great advantage in exploiting the favored status of these rent-a-car companies in Germany and contracted with them to buy their new models immediately.

Why would they sell to Gerhard?

Because there was a bonus structure for the rent-a-car companies. The more they bought, the bigger the bonus for them at the end of the year. This was very good for them. And, for Gerhard, the remarkable advantage was having the new models for sale in Austria before the Austrian dealerships could even touch them.

You can imagine how pissed the Mercedes dealers in Austria were. They hated "Grey Importers" like Gerhard and me. Mercedes Wiesenthal was the general importer for all of Austria and we were on its "destroyer list." They watched us like an eagle circling for the kill.

Wiesenthal may have wanted to kill us, but we were the real killers. You see, one of the characteristics of many Mercedes buyers was their enormous desire to trump their fellow enthusiasts by getting the first models before anyone else. These folks were willing to pay a premium price, often far more than the list price, to produce their trump card.

Of course, Gerhard, with his super aggressive trading tactics, created very powerful enemies in the car business, but he never appeared to give a damn.

Whatever virus Gerhard had, I must have caught it, too. Because I

SATURDAY AFTERNOON AND SUNDAY, I METAMORPHOSED INTO MR. WELL-BEHAVED FAMILY MAN.

didn't care what any of those mega-dealerships thought. With every new model changeover, we both made pretty good profits. In fact, together we sold hundreds of cars before the Austrian car dealerships could get them.

The Mercedes dealers hated us passionately and tried everything they could to stop us, but they couldn't do anything against us legally. Gerhard was located in Linz, about 120 miles away from my car lot. Pretty soon, we both acquired the reputation for having new Mercedes and BMWs earlier than the conventional dealerships. Soon, for good or for evil, we became legends in the Austrian car business. When they called us "Grey Zone Dealers," we just tipped our hats, pushed up our sunglasses, and smiled.

I was tremendously busy at this time, and my mind was always 100 percent focused on business. Still on Saturday afternoon and Sunday, I metamorphosed into Mr. Well-Behaved Family Man.

## Making My "Mark"

My parents and my brother as well as all my relatives, including Herta's parents, were skeptical about my astronomical ascent into prosperity, and, of course, it scared them. For conventionally positioned people, nothing scares them more than someone who is fearless about business and dares to believe in the possibilities for capitalism, particularly when functioning in the heart of a socialist economic system. For me, risk was an adventure. For them, risk was anathema.

Yes, they watched me grow and make lots of money, but none of them ever said, "Man, you are doing ever so great!" or "We are proud of your success and we can see that it is truly the product of your hard work." It was more like, "Oh my God, Hans, how can you think this will ever work? You will see! Something will happen!"

Like most young men, I always secretly wished that someone in my family would step up to the plate and compliment me on my success, but that never happened. Still, in a way, I think their reluctance to accept the reality of my success that was staring them in the face daily was a prime motivator for me to expand further ... to push my entrepreneurial instincts to the limit. I know it was childish, but I think I took some kind of secret pleasure at thumbing my nose at their irrepressible scorn at my ambition and achievements. It was the same feeling I had for our socialistic and totally entrepreneur hostile government.

Every six months I changed cars—moving from a Mercedes 500 to Mercedes 600 to the new BMWs, Porsches and beyond. There is euphoria about the upswing to success and I was young enough to believe in its vitality and permanence.

So, chastened by my relatives and friends, I stuck my success in their face, with these expensive cars, by ornamenting my fingers with diamond rings and my neck with gold chains. My attire was custom-fashioned from the best designer clothes and shoes hand-made in various European countries. In the cold Austrian winters, Herta and I both wore exquisite fur coats.

After work, I stopped at "in" places, had a couple of drinks, invited owners, managers and the "important," affluent patrons to my table, flirted with women shamelessly and loved all the attention I got as a consequence of my aggressive showmanship.

I wanted to be somebody in my town and in the surrounding area. Wherever I went, somebody knew me. I became a local celebrity. I didn't see my parents often, maybe once a month. They were still in the restaurant that they took over from my grand-parents, working their butts off. One day, I promised myself, I will go and open up that butcher shop and take over the restaurant, the vineyards, and the entire farm.

Still, despite my good intentions, I did not really help them out at all. I was too busy with myself. Eventually, I gave up the idea of taking on the project from my parents because it seemed so insignificant compared to my growing ambition for wealth and success.

My only real contact with my family took place when a relative had a birthday or there was a holiday like Easter and Christmas. Then I joined them, but that was it.

In 1976, my brother Franz married Traude, a seemingly nice lady. It was a huge wedding with 200 guests, and we celebrated until early in the morning. The affair reminded me that my time would come pretty soon.

Franz and Traude moved into Wiener Neustadt where Franz was living on the second floor, and I was still living on the first floor with Herta.

I think every boy secretly wants his father's approval. As actor Paul Newman said about his deceased father, "I would have liked to know that I could *cut the mustard.*" Unfortunately, Newman's father died before he became a super star. Newman not only cut the mustard, he built an empire out of salad dressing with the entire proceeds given to charity.

Yes, I longed for my father's approval, for his acknowledgment of who I was and what I was doing.

I loved my mother very much. When I sat down with her, she wanted to know what I was doing. I could chat with her about business and I think she understood me. But my dad, that was another thing altogether. When I told him I had made a killing in business or told him about my future dreams, his face would go blank. He'd tell me what he did in the vineyards that day or how many trees he had chopped down last week in our forest.

There was no connecting with me or what I was doing.

I WAS A DRUNKEN, VORACIOUS PARTY ANIMAL.

Even when I told him about a heartfelt problem, it was as though he could not hear a word I said. I tried hard and often, but never could make a dent in his completely stoic posture. It was like we were from different countries and one spoke Chinese, the other Farsi. It wasn't as though he hated or disliked what I was saying. It was as if, when I said something, I wasn't really there at all.

Despite living in the same house on different floors, Franz and I hardly had any contact at all. The few times we did, our conversations usually ended with stupid arguments. I had the sense that perhaps he was jealous of me. At the time, I was speeding down my sweet success road at two hundred miles an hour.

I was still in love with Herta. We were opposites in personalities—she was much more withdrawn than I was. When we were invited to parties, I was always laughing and drinking heavily, carrying on so to speak. Herta, on the other hand, stayed out of the spotlight. Several friends of mine told me that I was charming and funny, but she was boring, not something a prospective groom wants to hear about his bride-to-be. I was a drunken, voracious party animal and she was the prim and proper school teacher who dutifully went to parties because of her social obligations.

Life went on, but then suddenly took a strange turn.

One day, when I was on my car lot trying to sell a vehicle, I got terrible cramps in my stomach. I had to get on my knees, so intense was the pain—my first thought was that I ate something really bad.

Instinctively and perhaps stupidly, I headed to my office where I had a private bar for customers. Thinking it would settle my stomach, I poured myself two double shots of Jaegermeister. Instead of alleviating my cramps as I had hoped, I felt a sharp pain in my abdomen, like someone had rammed a knife in my stomach. Never in my life had I felt anything like that.

At that time, I had an employee whose mother was a nurse. He called her and described my pain. She quickly came to my office, and as soon as she saw me, she said, "You've got to go to the hospital immediately. Your eyes are completely yellow; you've got hepatitis."

My first reaction was very rude. Loudly, I said, "Bullshit," and stared down at some paperwork. I certainly didn't want that answer.

She practically had to push me into her car and then drove me to the emergency room. As we drove, my pain got worse and I was really glad that she had been so insistent.

Her diagnosis was right on target and, in an hour, I was told that I had hepatitis B, and the doctor told me I could infect other people. Being quarantined wasn't something that had ever entered my mind, but that's what happened as the doctor put me in a separate room.

# 14

# Hepatitis

*My mind kept racing.* Damn it! *I thought.*
Where the hell did this come from?

It was hard to believe. One moment I was enthusiastically building my business and the next moment, I was isolated in a bare hospital room. Quarantined.

The next day, I was given a battery of tests and duly informed that I was lucky to be alive. My liver was dreadfully poisoned and, if I had stayed one more day at home, I would have been beyond help. At that point, the liver poisoning would have been irreversible and I would have died of cirrhosis.

When I heard all this, I was shocked. How on earth could I have contracted hepatitis? There were many ways: from a person, from food like bad meat or raw eggs, etc. There was no telling unless they had more information.

I now had to stay in quarantine without any contact with the outside world. I had to pray, and hope the medication would

I LOVED TO WINE AND DINE, BUT SURVIVAL ALSO WAS IMPORTANT TO ME.

work and my liver could recover. There was no guarantee that it would.

My mind kept racing. *Damn it!* I thought. *Where the hell did this come from?* My nearest guess was a dish of beef tartare I had eaten in a restaurant a couple of days ago. Tartare is basically a slice of uncooked beef with a raw egg on the top. From what I knew, that was the only likely candidate, but right now, I was screwed. A few days ago, I had been incredibly busy in my office and had so much to do. Now I was isolated in a hospital room where no one could visit. I thought, shit, what should I do?

The answer was simple: nothing ... I could do nothing.

If it hadn't been for my worker's mother and her insistence that I get to a hospital immediately, I would have never gone. By now, I would have been dead or at death's door. It is hard to unravel the twists and turns of our destiny, especially when a slender thread could so easily yank us out of this world.

It took more than six weeks to be released. Then, I had to live with a very strict diet: no alcohol, no fatty foods, only grilled chicken, rice and salad, with everything only slightly seasoned. And I wasn't gobbling any beef tartare, believe me!

I had to be on this Spartan diet for a year and get a full checkup every month. I was told that if I didn't follow the rules strictly, my liver would never fully recover and I would have to deal with liver disease for the rest of my life. The way I felt, I didn't feel it would be for very long, anyway.

My preferred way of drinking and eating anything I wanted had to take a back burner to getting and staying well. I didn't fool around with my new diet or the checkups mandated by the doctors. The diet was particularly hard—I loved to wine and dine, as you may have noticed, but survival also was important to me ... I was determined to recover.

As a result of my determination, after one year, my liver had completely recovered.

The six-week hospital stay definitely impacted my business, but I survived that as well.

CHAPTER

# 15

# The Game Room Reinvented

*We had tasted blood and wanted to move fast,*
*but soon realized that it was not that easy.*

Around March of 1978, one of my customers offered me a location close to the railway station in Wiener Neustadt. The rent was so cheap I couldn't pass up the opportunity to look at it.

When I did, I drew a blank. Cheap, yes, but what could I do with it? I told him I would think about it and get in touch with him later.

For the moment, I was stymied, yet determined, somehow, to take advantage of the opportunity—I didn't want to make a promise until I had been able to assess it.

That same day I stopped outside the Airplane Bar and looked around. Siegi's Mercedes 500 SL was in the parking lot. Suddenly, bells and whistles went off in my mind.

I went right in and found Siegi, proposing to him that we should build a game room or arcade in that location near the railway station. A lot of kids took the train every day and you could see them milling around the station, waiting, doing nothing. Siegi was now quite experienced in maintaining his dad's

> WE WERE UNBELIEVABLY SUCCESSFUL AND SOON HAD A SENSE OF ITS POTENTIAL.

video games and slot machines. When I told him about the location, he became quite excited about the idea and promised he would take a look at the location the next day.

This he did. Within hours, he enthusiastically called me, affirming the value of the location and his wish to get started immediately. Without any hesitation, I made him a partner and together we formed Sitter & Holz, Inc. In less than three months, we opened up our first game room.

We were unbelievably successful and soon had a sense of its potential. In the first month, we earned cash—$18,000 after all expenses had been paid—and made a decision to find another place. We had tasted blood and wanted to move fast, but soon realized that it was not that easy. I was still working on my house. My auto shop was okay, but sales traffic was slower than I wanted it to be. I still had an overstocked inventory and bank loans with monthly payments.

And despite the promising performance during the first month, the game room near the railroad station cost us close to $300,000 dollars to get up and running. Both of us had put in money and Siegi had some extra cash, but now we both were running out of it.

Just because we had a nice profit and could make interesting and probably reliable forecasts of sales in the future, it didn't mean we could just hop on the rapid expansion wagon.

Smart business people, when they're stuck, retreat into analysis to find a solution. Although I may seem impulsive, even in my most rapid, expansionary moves, I always thought deeply about what I was doing. Sometimes, the responsibility and results were overwhelming. And more times than not, fate would intervene in both a positive and negative way. But, no matter what I did, at least I had a reason for it.

So we searched for another way to capitalize on the video game and slot machine business. Our research initially suggested that it might be a good idea to put slot machines in restaurants, gas stations and bars. So we tried, but every time we saw a suitable place, we found another vending company already positioned there with a contract allowing for a 50-50 split with the owner. Most of these contracts were iron-clad, netting them $20,000 to $40,000 a month, and stipulating a long-term agreement, usually from five to ten years.

MY CONCEPT AT THAT TIME WAS: "EVERYTHING OR NOTHING. HOP OR DROP!"

Even if we wanted to lease a space in a promising location, we couldn't seem to find one easily. Every time we came across a suitable location, there was a game room close by or the rent was prohibitive. We were disappointed, but still hungry for more.

And then, I had an idea.

"Look, Siegi," I told him while we were chatting in my office, "what if we change our plans slightly? What if instead of looking to build a game room, we decided to look for a restaurant. Then, we wouldn't have to split the money with a vendor like these other restaurants. And we could make money from it as well."

Siegi looked at me and smiled thoughtfully.

"And guess what?" I said. "It's going to be a helluva lot easier to get a permit."

Siegi smiled even more broadly.

So we agreed, but we still had a shortage of cash. And Siegi, despite his age, was much more conservative than I was. I had a large appetite for risk. My concept at that time was: "Everything or Nothing. Hop or Drop!"

In 1978, my brother and sister-in-law had a son. The family came together to celebrate, an increasingly rare event for me.

## My Clock Was Ticking

A year passed and, finally, in June 1979, I finished my house—around 3,500 square feet with a cellar and an open fireplace on the terrace in front of the living room. The interior was luxurious; the backyard was gorgeous and perfectly landscaped. It was pretty and expensive-looking.

This took us seven long years, working hard every single weekend, a mammoth accomplishment. We were both very proud of ourselves, but where had the time gone?

It was now clearly the time to get married, as we had planned from the beginning after the house was finally built.

I still loved Herta, but, after eight years, the fire had somewhat dwindled.

I didn't know what to do. I felt that our relationship lacked the same explosive, passionate promise it had held in the beginning. We were not really the same people who had fallen in love.

At this time, I was a full-blooded entrepreneur with a voracious appetite for success. The stars themselves loomed closer to me than other people in my acquaintance and I shocked everyone with my ferocious attitude toward the future.

As far as I was concerned, I owned the future—and nothing could stop me.

In retrospect, I would now temper many of my attitudes and beliefs with the wisdom of experience—of the ups and downs of the roller coaster—but I would never change. I have never changed that optimism I felt back then and my belief in my ability to succeed and prosper.

Wisdom is important, but it should never take the fire out of living. In that fire of hope is life itself—not just for me, but for everyone.

Then, and now, I loved the challenge of the life and the journey to overcome whatever obstacles were in my way. On the other hand, Herta, my future bride, as smart and nice as she was, was very conservative and shy. She still drove a little, used, VW Golf (which cost around 6,000 bucks). I was happy to give her another car, but she was scared of what the neighbors might say. My car was a Mercedes 500 SE, AMG tuned, and cost $120,000.

It was often parked conspicuously next to her VW. What did the neighbors think of that?

The scariest part of hooking up with Herta was having to observe her parents every day.

These people lived by the clock. Her father came home every day at exactly 5:00 PM. He had dinner promptly one hour later. At 7:00 PM, it was time for TV. Her father had an unwavering weekend routine. Saturday: he washed his car and did yard work. Sunday: he hiked in nearby forest.

In summer, her parents went to the same little hotel on the same little beach in the same little town in Italy that they had gone to for the last thirty years. Even their two-week vacation was invariable, fixed in heavenly cement by their permanent fixation with familiar schedules and familiar places.

They lived day-by-day, year-by-year, on the same relentless track of time. No challenges ... no highs ... no lows. Safe and secure in their prison of time.

CHAPTER

# 16

# Getting Married

*Then the moment came—that moment!*

Whether I liked my situation or not, our families, on both sides were eager to bring about this marriage. And despite the numbing slowness of our parents in almost every other respect, they handled the marriage arrangements with lightning speed and dexterity.

Holy Moly! It was really going to happen. The date for our official marriage was set on August 11, 1978. And considering the size of both of our families, it was going to happen in a big way.

⌒

The wedding itself was going to take place in the Dome of the beautiful Catholic Church in Wiener Neustadt, the ceremony and mass celebrated by the Bishop himself. Three hundred people were invited and my friends ordered a white coach pulled with four white horses. It was going to be a Cinderella wedding.

Prior to the ceremony, Herta and I had to take a two-week evening class in preparation for a Catholic marriage. This was supposed to teach us what marriage was all about.

One week before the wedding, my friends sprung for a bachelor party at the Airplane Bar. I got really drunk. At exactly midnight, again organized by my thoughtful friends, two call girls showed up. I was told later that they were paid to quasi-rape me.

I am not quite sure what that really meant, and, believe me, I didn't press hard for a description. The reality is that I had absolutely no recollection of what happened. I passed out in the middle of our celebration and woke up the next day on a couch in the Airplane Bar's office.

Finally, the big day came. There was a mandatory appearance at City Hall for the license at 11:00 AM and the local newspaper showed up. The next day we were on the front page.

My best men were Vick Maier, my mechanic and Karl Andritz, my friend who handled our car parts at Rothmund's in Vienna. We all had lunch together and the marriage itself would take place at 3:00 PM in the Dome.

When I picked up Herta at her parents' house, she was crying. When I first saw her, tears also came to my eyes. She seemed so extraordinarily lovely that day, beautiful in her white wedding dress and veil.

I thought how much I still loved her. We had been together for eight years already. Our ceremony would be like icing on the wedding cake.

City Hall was located smack in the middle of downtown Wiener Neustadt. And as we approached the building, we could see an elegant white coach with four gleaming white horses waiting to give us the final fairy tale touch to our marital ceremony. By the time we got there, spectators lined the street, waiting for a glimpse of the bride and groom—Herta and me!

As we ascended the coach, the crowd lining up and down the streets, a few from time to time yelling out our names or loudly wishing us well. we could hear murmuring in the crowd. The coach then slowly headed in the direction of the Dome.

BY NOW, ALL MY CONCERNS AND DOUBTS WERE LULLED INTO A SOFT, ALMOST IMPERCEPTIBLE HUM IN THE BACK OF MY MIND.

Then the moment came—that moment! We were in the Church and Herta's father brought her to me, while the Bishop stood before us, ready to preside over the ceremony. In the background, you could hear "Ave Maria" softly sung by the choir as the organ spun out its rich chords.

There could have been no better storybook wedding. Or, if you preferred another drama, it would make a touching ending to a dynastic soap opera season. It was beautiful, even majestic, but, unfortunately, more a gorgeous mirage than a fitting tribute to a lasting union.

Still, when we repeated the words from the Bishop to confirm our faith and loyalty to each other, when we put the rings on each other's finger and said the final "I do," we were both completely sincere, I am sure. By now, all my concerns and doubts were lulled into a soft, almost imperceptible hum in the back of my mind.

Everybody in the Dome had teary eyes and some were actually sobbing. It was a beautiful, memorable wedding.

Of course, the real fun and camaraderie of a wedding is the reception afterward. Accordingly, we all trooped over to a restaurant which treated everyone to live music and a five course feast. We were with all our relatives, friends and guests—more than 250 people showed up.

It is traditional for the relatives of the married couple to bake a ton of cookies for this celebration, and every guest who came left with a box of homemade cookies. Every guest, again, according to tradition, had to dance with the bride or the groom and afterward, perhaps the most welcome part of the tradition is that they would put money in a top hat to help the newly married couple after the dance. It was expected that this money would finance the honeymoon or help them move into their new dwelling.

Our wedding party lasted until 5:00 AM. When the last guest left, Herta and I could barely walk as our feet were aching from dancing all night. We were glad to have our parents help us put all the flowers and the presents in two cars. An extra car was necessary because all the presents couldn't fit into the car that held the bride and groom.

To make matters even more exciting, when we counted the money in the top hat, we found $38,000, a damn good present for any freshly married couple.

Finally, we drove home, exhausted beyond all expectations. Still, when we got to the door, I carried her over the threshold and gave her a long, intense kiss. We then both fell straight into the bed and had just enough energy to take off our clothes before passing out. A kiss on the threshold was all we got that evening, but it was a very good kiss.

CHAPTER

17

# Expansion

*One of the side effects of the entrepreneurial "sickness"
is that once the good times roll, there is the tendency
to become addicted to the perceived trend of profitability.*

That was our first night together in our new house.

When Herta and I woke up, we moved quickly into the shower. There we embraced, kissed each other passionately and made furious love under the hot water.

After finishing our lovemaking, we sat down with the shower still running and licked the water drops from each other's lips. We sat there a long time, holding hands and looking into each other's eyes. With the water cooling, we finally left the shower, put on comfortable clothes and had our first breakfast alone in the house that we built together.

After breakfast, we went straight back to the bedroom, falling in each other's arms, hugging and kissing each other desperately, relentlessly, celebrating our belated wedding night once again with feverish intensity. Then, exhausted from our first rendezvous in our own bedroom in our own house, we fell back to sleep.

It was the doorbell's persistent ring, I guess, that woke us up. It was the middle of the afternoon ... who in the hell was invading the privacy of our first honeymoon hours?

It turned out to be Herta's parents ... and now, awake and somewhat satiated with our lovemaking, we were actually glad to see them. Opening our door, we acceded to their kind offer to help us with the wonderful pile of presents that cascaded all over our living and dining room. It was really a major task and despite our appreciation for all the presents, was not a time we wanted to bother with the hours needed to devote to such a mundane chore.

Being tired from our first sex adventure at home, we took it easy and let her parents do most of the opening and organizing and documenting, helping out in a laggardly way.

Then everything was in order and Herta's mom prepared dinner. After that, we went to bed again, but this time to get a good night's sleep.

In two days, we would leave for our honeymoon in Crete, a beautiful island in Greece. Meanwhile, I had to organize my business to accommodate my two week's absence. This was not easy. I was tied up every moment before we left.

We thought that Crete, the largest of the Greek islands, would be an ideal place for a honeymoon. We booked the Astir Palace Elounda, a deluxe hotel and bungalow resort. It was located between the colorful fishing village of Elounda and Aghious Nikolaos.

Our room had its own terrace overlooking the hotel's two private beaches and swimming pool. You could take your pick of

ONE MOMENT WE WERE
TENSE, FOCUSED ADULTS.
THEN, WE WERE KIDS
PLAYING IN THE SAND.

all kinds of watery adventures—gazing at a submerged ancient city, taking a sailing trip, snorkeling, or scuba diving. You could take your lunch on the shaded terrace and enjoy the majestic view.

If you had worked as hard as we had, you can imagine the thrill and even shock of suddenly being liberated from the shackles of work. Oh, I loved work, but I found that playing with Herta was just as much fun, especially since, at that time, our hearts and souls seemed like one.

One moment we were tense, focused adults. Then, we were kids playing in the sand, swimming, wind surfing, building sand castles like big kids with nothing else to do except relax and have fun.

In the day, sometimes we would just lay there, absorbing the sun and our freedom-starved bodies. In the evening, we went dancing, but soon headed to the bedroom, falling to sleep each night after a maddening vortex of probing, embracing, kissing, as we plumbed the depths of our love for each other. It was fourteen days of paradise.

As the days shot by, I lost my skepticism about Herta entirely. The background noise in my mind vanished, and I thought it was, in fact, the right thing to get married after eight years. The intense lovemaking and feverish hunger we had for each other proved we had what it took to be a happy couple, from now until the end of our lives. I now really believed in our love. I thought that destiny had not abandoned us.

## My Lust Redirects to Expansion

When we came back home, my work began at first in a mad drive to catch up, but then in an even more mad drive to push ahead, to sweep aside all obstacles and grow my businesses with even greater audacity and conviction.

Siegi and I finally found a location in Eisenstadt and opened up a small restaurant called Café Harlequin with a separate game room where we placed 20 slot machines. You could win serious cash in Café Harlequin if you were lucky, and a lot of our regular restaurant patrons frequented the game room. Harlequin became the seed of a franchise that we decided to mount in other locations.

> AT FIRST I WAS ARROGANT, THEN I BECAME INTELLIGENTLY AMBITIOUS BUT THEN FINALLY, I BECAME LIKE A CONFIDENT NAVIGATOR.

The first test of duplication took place six months later in Moedling, a little town close to Vienna. We also installed 20 slot machines there.

We now had a game room in Wiener Neustadt with 60 games and two Café Harlequins. Soon, we were taking in about $60,000 to $80,000 profit monthly from three profitable locations.

One of the side effects of the entrepreneurial "sickness" is that once the good times roll, there is the tendency to become addicted to the perceived trend of profitability, thinking that this particular wave will never stop, that you have finally found the true, unrelenting cash generator, the fountain of money that will last forever.

Now, as an inveterate entrepreneur, I am joking a bit when I call entrepreneurship a sickness, because it can be and is, for me, a great blessing. But not when it is laden with the "Fantasy of Foreverness."

An entrepreneur has to be as ready to jump ship as he is to board one. This is how he turns the instinct for profitability into a long-term pattern of success by noting when the tide is going out, as well as when the tide is coming in. However, I was becoming somewhat dizzy from this new twist of success.

On the next October 26th—on Herta's birthday, to be exact—I bought her a Porsche. But, instead of being delighted, she was shocked and befuddled. She brought up the sad litany about what the neighbors would think (something I would never, ever give a shit about). Still, after she drove around a bit and thought about it, her middle-class fears began to abate and she became accustomed to the idea that she had made it to the land of the wealthy, and deserved to live it and have fun.

For myself, I have always enjoyed wealth, but I have learned now that physical wealth and its trappings is a very fragile commodity compared to the wealth we have inside. I think that true wealth is a reflection of what we have inside us—and that the wealth of a Saint Theresa and a Gandhi might be as true as the wealth of a Warren Buffet or a Bill Gates.

There are men and women who can rightfully enjoy the trappings of wealth because that is their rightful destiny. But, there are those whose wealth is a reflection of their shabby, uncontrollable lust after the things of the world for themselves, and that can be, in itself, very twisted.

That is why, when I have been broke and began to realize this great truth—that the wealth is inside me—that I became much more fearless, knowing that I had the ability to create true wealth because of my inward connection to some great truth that lay entirely in my own consciousness. At first I was arrogant, then I became intelligently ambitious, but then finally I became like a confident navigator. While to others, I might appear to be lost in an ocean of confusion, to myself, I was convinced that with a little time, I would find the proper configurations of stars that would lead me to the next level of prosperity. And I did—again and again.

I'm not sure where the Hunt brothers stood on this scaffolding of success, but throughout the world they successfully created an unbelievable silver boom and became a synonym for successful wealth creation.

In the last quarter of 1979, the price of silver went through the roof. At this time, Austria's ten schilling coin contained 97 percent fine silver. Its coin literally exploded in value.

Before the boom, the coin had a value of about one dollar, but now you could go to any coin dealer and get back three or four dollars where the bank would only pay you one dollar. During 1979 and 1980, Siegi and I literally doubled, no tripled, our income by trading this coin.

Destiny had laid this opportunity on our doorstep because all of our slot machines operated with a 10 schilling coin, so each day we could triple and quadruple their value in real dollars just by a simple visit to the coin dealers.

One day, when Karl Andritz came to visit me, I took him with me to our game rooms and he helped me empty all our machines with the silver 10 schilling coins.

It was hard work and we could barely carry the full buckets to my car. When we finally got the six buckets in the back seat, the rear end of the car was beginning to plunge toward the street. With my car very much overloaded, I had to drive very slowly for fear of destroying it.

Karli was simply amazed and was laughing during our entire adventure. We carried the heavy buckets to the coin vendor and cashed them in. He felt, like I did, that he had temporarily moved to another world.

In January 1980, silver reached its highest point, climbing to $50 an ounce. Three months later, the crash came and by March of that year, one ounce of silver dropped to $21 an ounce. I can't say I was as prepared for this intellectually as I should have been, but Siegi and I still lucked out because we had consistently cashed our schillings in. So, without holding any inventory to speak of in silver, the drop didn't affect our assets at all. It could have, though.

In fact, soon afterward, the government took the 10 schilling coin out of its official currency and the big boom was terminated forever. And while Siegi and I made a few hundred thousand dollars from the silver boom, the Hunt brothers, who engineered it all, went completely broke and wound up being prosecuted.

## The Silver Lining Dulls

Remember how I said that an entrepreneur should be wary, and be ready to step out of a losing game? Well, my education in that kind of smart business strategy was accelerated when, at the end of 1979, an oil crisis occurred in the midst of the Iranian Revolution. Unfortunately, at the same time, my car business took a big hit.

During the early part of 1979, amid massive protests, the Shah of Iran, Mohammad Reza Pahlavi, fled his country, allowing the Ayatollah Khomeini to gain control. The protests shattered the Iranian oil sector.

While the new regime resumed oil exports, the quantity was inconsistent and at a lower volume. Prices accordingly went up. This triggered a widespread panic. In 1980, following the Iraqi invasion of Iran, oil production in Iran nearly stopped, and Iraq's oil production was severely cut as well.

New oil was very scarce and gasoline prices became very high. So to conserve the supply of gasoline, the government of Austria created "car free days." Each car had a sticker on its windshield, stamped with the "car free" date. On that day, if you were foolish enough to drive, you would be ticketed by the police.

You can imagine what this did to the car business in Austria. My own car sales dropped dramatically. Every single sale necessitated a trade-in, so I had to cut prices for cash-starved owners. As a consequence, my inventory moved quickly from 120 to 150 used cars. All my cash and profit was safely parked on my parking lot, tied up in trade-ins.

Although I had, for a time, rested somewhat comfortably in my present situation, I gradually realized that I could actually go under because of lack of cash. Still, Siegi and I were consistently making money with our game room and two cafés.

It is particularly disturbing to see one business rising while the other business falls, thereby jeopardizing growth and security. I thereby embarked on a new strategy.

Early on, I had found a half acre lot on Highway 17 in Vienna. Thinking ahead, I had leased that property with the right to buy it within a period of five years.

My idea was to put Mercedes, BMWs and exclusive sports cars on that lot. I hoped that the sales in Vienna would cover my losses, but my gamble went awry. Slowly, everything I made with Siegi began to just cover my losses in the car business.

CHAPTER

# 18

# Another Chance

*My God! What an idea! Inwardly I more than smiled,
but outwardly I maintained my composure.*

It was time to bail, but how?

One day, I was surprised to find Helmut Schaerf in my office. Remember, we didn't go into business together because our wives didn't liked each other. No, that's the wrong description, they despised each other. We both said, "Fuck that shit. It will not work at all." And from that day on, we had little connection. Looking back, I still believed his wife couldn't compare to my Herta. I admit she was beautiful but a really demanding and arrogant bitch—nothing was ever good enough. I was kind of sorry for him and I suspect that maybe at times, he was thinking the same about me and my wife—that Herta was the problem.

But as I knew, sometimes he hung out with my friends barhopping and just fooling around. Overall, I thought he was a nice guy and very talented but it was not our destiny in that time to create something together or work together.

Imagine my surprise when he came by and politely offered me a deal that could potentially save my business!

Helmut used to be in the car business like me, when we decided to go our own ways but he then procured a bar and dance club in Mattersburg, a little town with a population of maybe 15,000, about 20 miles from Wiener Neustadt. And he did well in the business.

Why on earth would he offer me a deal?

"As you know, Hans," he said, "when you own this type of business, there are a lot of temptations. And whether you take them or not, you are always up late anyway, and the night life is killing my relationship with my wife."

My first thought was, *Oh here we go, I knew your wife is a nightmare and a bitch and you should have listened to me that time,* but I said not one word.

"That's terrible," I said, "but what has that got to do with me?"

"I want to get back into the car business."

"Do you really think that's a good idea? I mean—now—with the price of gas, cars are no longer the premium item in the marketplace."

"I know that, Hans, but everything that goes up, goes down ... and then," he said, smiling, "probably goes up again. So, in my opinion, in the long run, cars will go up again, and I can hold out. Can you?"

"You have a point there, my friend. What's your idea?"

"I could sell the bar for $300,000, but I think I might do better just trading it for the cars that I would buy anyway, to get back into the business. So, why don't you let me trade my bar for some of this extravagant used inventory?"

My God! What an idea! Inwardly I more than smiled, but outwardly I maintained my composure. "Sounds good, but I would like to see your bar and the real estate first before we go any further."

Helmut said, "No problem my friend, I understand and we can do that tomorrow."

DESPITE MY NEW WAVE OF SUCCESS, I FELT A GREAT DEAL OF STRESS IN MY LIFE.

The next day, I drove over to Mattersburg and, from the first moment I saw the place, I knew I wanted it. Not only was business good, it was an ideal location for slot machines!

Accordingly, Helmut chose 25 premium used cars from my lot. So I became an owner of another bar and disco that I quickly refurbished, and changed the name to the "Meeting Point." Soon we were ready for a grand opening.

During this period, I began to take Herta with me on the weekends, often in the evenings, to visit my various holdings. In this way, I could maintain a vigilant watch over my properties, touch base with the managers, chat with customers and spend some time with her. Business people often enjoy having a relationship with the owners and managers of restaurants and bars, so I made my presence part of the ambiance of the locations.

But, despite my new wave of success, I felt a great deal of stress in my life. Like a candle that had maintained its bright flame for years and years, I was slowly burning out. My remedy was to take on some kind of rigorous activity—a sport, perhaps.

I needed it. I felt out of shape and I had gained weight. For me, neither was acceptable.

I was not looking for something that was easy—I was looking for something challenging and maybe even useful. I chose Jiu Jitsu, focusing on self-defense. My business objective was always to be able to take down somebody fast and economically with no meaningless flourishes or showy insubstantial moves. Focusing on self-protection made my new sport more serious. In fact, it got my mind off business and into the challenging world of a sport that involved personal physical survival.

For the same reason, I also began to go to a shooting range for training in firearms.

Shortly after my training, I filed for a license to carry a 38 special Smith & Wesson. Along with my Jiu Jitsu training, having a firearm provided me with another layer of protection because I handled a lot of cash every day. From the day I received the license, I carried the pistol on my belt wherever I went.

Jiu Jitsu was my protection policy for my businesses, but as I revealed, I had gained a lot of weight over the years and my challenge was to get some of this weight off and get fit. I needed to take up a strenuous recreational sport. I started to play tennis, adding it to my weekly routine and worked out with a trainer four hours a week.

I signed up just two miles from my car lot. Kramer's Tennis and Squash Center was an indoor tennis and squash center with a nice little restaurant attached. It belonged to two brothers, Gerhard and Franz Kramer.

Next to the sports center, the Kramers owned a factory where they produced their unique, patented fire hydrants. They had built the center for their own use, in a convenient location, treating the business part of it as a means of supporting their favorite recreational activities.

During this time, I liked Gerhard Kramer but I had difficulty appreciating his brother, Franz, but became good friends with Gerhard. My friend, Ferrence, who I saw a lot of was also friends with them and often we would play tennis doubles.

The summers are pretty short in Austria. The winters, on the other hand, are far too long. That was the reason I chose indoor tennis, but it was expensive.

In order to take maximum advantage of the opportunity, you had to have reservations for the full year. Soon after I started, Herta began to play too. At $20 an hour, a hefty fee in those days, this made Herta's and my chosen sport more of an "investment."

I met a lot of people while playing and I began to love tennis, not only for the sport, but for the connections I made.

At the center one day, I met Anton Duda. After my training session, we had a beer together and made arrangements to play tennis together the next day. I lost, but we liked each other and agreed from then on to play every Friday from 5:00 to 7:00 PM, making sure we could reserve a court for that time.

Anton was working for the Austrian socialist oil production company. He made a $7,000 monthly salary and plenty of time to do whatever he liked. He had very powerful job protection with his contract, roughly translated from the German as a "Tenure-Track Position Agreement." This meant, essentially, he could not be fired unless he did something totally ridiculous, or conspicuously broke the law. It was a guaranteed lifetime job with a retirement plan.

After a couple of weeks, I invited Anton to go to dinner with me at the Meeting Point after our Friday match. As we walked through the front door, I could see he was quite impressed with my house. Herta then appeared and I introduced them to her.

I had to make a few stops along the way to check my properties, then we headed out to my Meeting Point restaurant. Arriving, the Disco was packed. Nonetheless, a lot of my friends and customers came up to me, hugging me warmly. Finally, my manager made it through the crowd and escorted us to a spot in the corner that was always reserved for me and any guests I had brought along. Afterward, we headed back to my house to have one last nightcap.

At that point, I could see that Anton was quite impressed by my lifestyle, my relationship with Herta, and all my various holdings.

My guess is that, although he never really talked about it, Anton was bored to death with his job. It was probably no challenge for him anymore, and the daily, monotonous routine was killing his spirit. Anton loved the adventurous lifestyle I lived and seemed to even enjoy my stories about the risks I would take to accomplish my goals.

Although Anton had total job security, could leave his job whenever he liked and had a very good salary, he still seemed to admire me and my rich, frantic lifestyle.

That, of course, was Anton's perspective.

On the other hand, Herta's perspective was quite different. In her view, Anton had a level of worldly intelligence and sophistication that clearly trumped my grasp of reality. Compared to Anton, my thinking and my language were crude and common.

I admit to the language critique. Mine was often crude. Frankly, I peppered my thinking and observations with a lot of hard-edged profanity.

As far as I was concerned, profanity like this is almost a business necessity when you are in the cultures of nightclubs, slot machines and selling high-powered, prestige vehicles, where you dealt with mechanics, rough-and-tumble car dealerships and street smart customers every day. Furthermore, I could drop the profanity and customize my language to a specific banker whenever I wanted. If I needed to speak to a potential investor, loan officer at a bank, or a government official, I could switch on what Americans might call an Ivy League demeanor, and chat it up without one swear word, in a soft, angelic voice that would shock anyone who might try to pigeonhole me with some kind of blue-collar identity.

> I WAS A SOCIAL CHAMELEON AND PROUD OF MY ADAPTABILITY.

In one day, I could speak to anyone with any title, whether royalty, executive or university professor, or a member of a street gang, and adapt the right tone and the right voice. I was a social chameleon and proud of my adaptability. It is not an uncommon talent. Most experienced sales people know how to adapt to the cultural background and temperament of their clients. Like me, they operate from an instinctive level, and like fine actors, choose their roles carefully.

The problem was that when I was at home or in a familiar environment with friends, I tried to more or less forget all that and be myself. And frankly, I did not see anything wrong with being a little bit loose with my language or casual with my observations. I did not want to have to dress up with my friends when enjoying some drinks or lying beside a swimming pool chatting about our lives and work.

But Anton was not that way. He did not need to adapt to anything but government service. And he had a suave and relaxed way of presenting things in a calm, intelligent manner. He never used any of the street smart nuances that flavored my approach and my sense of humor, his clearly giving him considerable credit in Herta's eyes.

I had no desire whatsoever to modify my behavior when I was relaxing with my wife and friends. They were supposed to like me for who I was—not for the roles I could affect.

I refused to be someone else, whether with Anton or anyone else, and this did not afford me a lot of favor with Herta.

Despite Anton's alleged superiority in handling life, he sure liked to hang around with me. It seemed that he dropped in daily at my car business, almost becoming a fixture of my workplace. I suspected that he was bored.

After tennis on Friday, we became a threesome—he was always with Herta and me, accompanying us on my route to check on various game rooms and restaurants, culminating in dinner. Considering the fact that he was married and had two children, it was amazing how he managed to hang around us as much as he did.

Anton was eleven years my senior and must have had a lot of responsibilities. He lived on the north side of Vienna, in Deutsch Wigram, almost two hours away from where we lived.

He was a commuter and his place of work was only ten minutes away from my main office on the car lot. Sometimes, on Friday when it was too late or inconvenient to go home, he slept in our guest room. He then left Saturday morning for home.

CHAPTER

# 19

# Venice

*Anytime I went there, I would always be magically
transported into a different cultural perspective
and a different period of time.*

$B$ack then, I was crazy enough to sometimes jump in my car and
drive 350 miles to Venice, which I absolutely loved. I could sit on
the Piazza San Marco, the main square of the city, surrounded by
chic sidewalk cafés, expensive boutiques and other fancy shops,
and drink an espresso watching life pass by.

At that time, I was not planning on becoming a writer, but I
think I had a novelist's view of things. I loved to watch everything
that was going on around me. I took mental notes about the
scenery, the restaurants, the people, their appearance, habits of
dress, the way they spoke to each other, their preferred choices
of dining and absorbed any chance encounter with a stranger.
These observations enriched my life and had a practical consequence

when I did business with widely divergent types of people. But I think it was also an aesthetically and culturally enriching experience.

When I finally decided to write about my life, I realized this habit of mine could bring a profound depth to my storytelling.

In Venice you had to pay a top price for whatever was on the menu just to sit at an outdoor table during the day, but in the evening there was entertainment—you could listen to live music too.

I loved Italy, the temperament and attitude of its people and their serious love of good food—tempting cuisine. I began to think seriously of buying a yacht and finding a slip in Grado, a tiny fishing village close to Venice but also very near the Austrian border.

Then there is Venice. It's hard to explain how much I loved this amazing city. With its colorful, traffic-free cobblestone streets which lay beside its one hundred fifty lovely winding canals, there is no finer place for walking in a city, and no greater romantic destination for a traveler seeking history and cultural enrichment at every step in his or her journey. There are 117 separate islands that make up Venice, and they are linked together with more than 400 bridges, often quite tiny and quaint in appearance.

With the magnificent churches and palaces around every corner, lively squares filled with interesting visitors and shops filled with fascinating curios of this wonderful place, and unique and expensive gifts for every taste and purpose that its shopping delivers, who wouldn't fall in love with it?

The Grand Canal is like Main Street in many cities, cutting and weaving through the heart of the city.

Anytime I went there, I would always be magically transported into a different cultural perspective, a different period of time, an ancient world of

architectural splendor, an historical kaleidoscope of mankind's triumphs and the tragic flaws of cities, kings and popes.

During my many visits, I either would sit in one of the little cafés or go to Harry's Bar, a watering hole for every trendsetter visiting in this and the last century. Giuseppe Cipriani, the esteemed founder of Harry's, was the alleged inventor of the Bellini. I would sip this sumptuous, internationally-known tall drink, named for its pink color resembling the toga of a saint painted in the 15th century by Giovanni Bellini. No doubt its peachy taste and sparkling Prosecco had cooled the palates of the great literary, artistic, cultural and Hollywood elite like writer Ernest Hemmingway, actor Charlie Chaplin, director Alfred Hitchcock, the Baron Philippe de Rothschild, industrialist Aristotle Onassis and so many others. Just being there made me feel like an intimate of the rich, powerful and famous. It's amazing what a little peach purée and sparkling wine can do for a visitor to Harry's Bar. It certainly did wonders for me and my imagination.

Despite the formidable distance and dangers of leaving my daily routine, I considered my trips to Venice an essential part of my lifestyle, a motivator to achieve greater vistas of success and satisfaction with the richness of my life.

One day, during a time when Herta was on her school break, but I was still in my office, Anton came by to visit me. When he entered my office, the first thing I said was, "Hey, Anton, what would you say if we picked up my wife and took a little drive for an espresso and a Bellini at Harry's Bar?"

"Harry's Bar? You mean the one in Venice?"

"Absolutely, my friend."

"Isn't that a bit extravagant?" He thought I was joking.

"Yes, it is," I said, turning to my secretary, Christa. "I need you to take care of things for a few days."

Minutes later, we jumped in my Mercedes 500 SEL and picked up Herta and we were on our way. Anton appeared dazed, as if he was dreaming, both astonished and incredulous at what we were doing when by early evening, he was sitting with us in a café at the "Piazza San Marco" and listening to songs of the Gondoliers. Later, while toasting each other over a couple of Bellinis and a bottle of champagne, he told me how much he admired me and my life. Herta heard him as he told me what a great life I had, how I seemed to be truly happy, full of energy and a zest for life.

Yes, she heard him, but did she really understand? And, I never knew if he had called his wife to let her know he would be gone for a few days.

CHAPTER

# 20

# Take Over

*"Life at full throttle" and "Enjoy the ride"*
*were my slogans.*

$A$t the end of 1980, my parents told me they'd like to semi-retire and asked me to take over the restaurant. They said they would still like to take care of the vineyards, the wheat fields, and the farm. And, I told them I would take over if they would agree with my conditions. So I made a deal with them.

I would invest in and refurbish the restaurant, providing them $2,000 a month for life. They would still have the income from the vineyards and the wheat fields, mother's retirement money from the government and now an additional $2,000 from me. That way they wouldn't have to be worried about money anymore. They agreed and we formalized it with a contract.

I completely remodeled one of the dining rooms, transforming it into a game room and a café with a small bar in the back. I invested at least $500,000 in the property and hired a married couple as managers.

I WAS IN HEAVEN. WHEN I TALLIED THE THREE POSITIONS, I MADE ABOUT A $50,000 TO $60,000 PROFIT MONTHLY.

Soon, it was making enough money to cover the expenses but I did not see one dollar of profit from the restaurant side. However, the slot machines delivered a pure profit of $30,000 a month—that made me really happy. In fact, my entire empire was beginning to prosper.

It had become a definite strain. But still, I was making an average of $30,000 monthly with Siegi and the Meeting Point. Now, after my investment in the restaurant from my parents and putting in a game room, the combination delivered a monthly profit of at least $20,000 to $30,000.

I was in heaven. When I tallied the three positions, I made around $50,000 to $60,000 profit monthly.

Next to our house was a half-acre for sale that I bought for the express purpose of enhancing our lifestyle. The addition allowed me to add an indoor swimming pool, a steam room, a sauna with a Jacuzzi, and a fitness center. It was like a little hotel.

When I started with construction, my in-laws, as usual, were more than skeptical. But when I finally was finished, and I invited them to a grand opening with 40 guests, there is no way to describe their shocked perplexity. But, by that point, their expressions of incredulity only added to my enjoyment. It was absolutely wonderful.

Prior to driving to the office in the morning, my day now started with a quick jump in the heated pool, summer or winter.

"Life at full throttle" and "Enjoy the ride" were my slogans.

At the beginning of 1981, I had a brainstorm. I wanted to create a beer pub with a new variety of draft beer, a small menu with very special sausages, and a couple of other really great tasting things to eat and, for sure, slot machines—some, but not many—maybe six to ten games. It would be an attempt to create a small, efficient, money-making bar with slots and games. I would call it "Kruegerl," which roughly translates to "Beer Mug."

I opened the first one in a walking zone in the center of Wiener Neustadt. Four months later, I opened one in Neunkirchen, another little town about twenty miles away. I made money, but I spent it fast on the expansion. In fact, I put everything I had into it.

Siegi became alarmed, saying, ""Hans, slow down! Why are you expanding so fast? Save some of your money and don't invest every penny that you make." My answer usually was, "Why? I love what I'm doing!"

SINCE MY OPERATIONS AND MY OWN GROWTH WERE CLEARLY VISIBLE, IT WAS NO SURPRISE THAT I WAS ONE OF THEIR FIRST TARGETS.

A couple of my friends gave me the same advice, but I was not listening to anyone in those days. As you can imagine from my attitude back then, I was always in the mood for anything that would accelerate the expansion of my businesses. I was on the hunt for any opportunity. And then, as though someone was listening, a way of further expanding just dropped into my lap.

At that time, there was a bank in Wiener Neustadt called Country Bank. They were small, but very aggressive and wanted to grow fast, just like me. And to accomplish their own expansionary plans, Country Bank replaced their old management team with a group of serious, sales-oriented bankers who were hungry to get loans.

Since my operations and my own growth were clearly visible, it was no surprise that I was one of their first targets. So when they approached me, suggesting they could help finance the next couple of restaurants, I was happy to share my numbers with them. They liked them and the deal was on.

To that end, I bought three different restaurants in Vienna, two of them fantastically positioned on the Ringstrasse. Most buildings on the Ringstrasse were designed for the middle and upper class. There were a lot of beautiful and famous buildings within it: the Parliament, the City Hall, the University, the Opera House, different museums, the famous gothic Votiv Church, as well as beautiful parks. On one side was the Danube Canal, a tributary of the Danube, and there was the detour through the city. Along the Ringstrasse, electric trams run; the U Bahn is the underground subway system, that runs under it. The First District is the area enclosed by the Ringstrasse and closed to all motorized traffic. The Ringstrasse and the First District are the premiere tourist destinations in Vienna, a city made up of 23 districts, of which the Ringstrasse and the enclosed Old City is number one.

I rented the spaces, paying for the three lease contracts, $2.4 million, and refurbished them for at least $800,000. The funny part was, with the $2.4 million-dollar obligation, I physically owned nothing; I just took over the grandfathered lease agreements.

Nevertheless, the bank loaned me $2.5 million for the entire deal.

I turned each of these restaurants into a Beer Mug, utilizing exactly the same concept as the other Beer Mugs in my line-up— with one important exception. Normally, I would put ten slots in each of them, but the local laws in Vienna forbade me doing that. You were only allowed to have five or six machines in a restaurant.

Now I had three Beer Mugs in Vienna, two Beer Mugs in lower Austria, one Disco and Bar in Mattersburg and one restaurant from my parents in Oslip. I also had my main car lot and main office in Theresienfeld, hosting many of my imported cars as well as a very productive body and repair shop. In addition to the main car lot, I had a sales outlet in Vienna that only dealt in super prestigious, expensive cars.

To cope with all this, I had to start my day quite early. I felt under more stress than I had ever experienced in my life. But I was determined to persevere and never thought about quitting, even for one minute.

My biggest problems were developing a system to properly manage all these restaurants and the unbelievably high cost of taxes in Austria. I was certainly making enough cash to brag about, but with the dwindling profitability of the car business, the loan itself began to become difficult to pay and meet my expenses as well.

In keeping with my philosophy of the time, when in doubt, expand. Take more risk, then cover losses with more profitability. To that end, I bought another restaurant with a huge disco in

Oggau, a little town in Burgenland. It became my second Meeting Point location. Now I had two chains: the Meeting Point and the Beer Mug.

I also bought another restaurant and disco in Wolkersdorf, north of Vienna. We called the disco another Meeting Point, now number three.

It also had a huge game room and a little gas station. This location was a gold mine. The game room itself produced at least $40,000 in net profit.

This was all great, but the Wolkersdorf position cost me $1.5 million. By the end of 1982, I was in debt by nine million to Country Bank in Wiener Neustadt—quite a chunk of money. Although it was a daunting amount to owe, I considered the debt just a slightly larger chip in a poker game that it was my destiny to play.

Leverage your debt to expansion and profitability wasn't something I made up. It was the essence of a certain type of entrepreneurship, sometimes staggeringly successful.

As I was now wishing to match my entrepreneurship with an enhanced lifestyle, I bought my first yacht in March of 1983. It was a used Riva 34-foot motor yacht that I acquired from a jeweler who I had met in Vienna. It cost me $80,000 and made me feel like a king.

As I had fantasized doing years before, I put the little yacht in Grado, that perfect little fishing village in Italy, close to the Austrian border. It was true that I had no idea when I would have the time to use it, but it was there, a clear sign that dreams can really come true.

My wife only saw me on the tennis court and on Friday nights, when we went with Anton to a nice restaurant, followed by a visit to one of my discos. The only change in the routine was the number of places I had to visit—more numerous, shorter and to the point. During the week, I still stopped at various popular locations on my way home, had a drink or two, flirted a bit and came home around 10 or 11 PM. Often, Herta was asleep by then.

By this time, Herta's best friend was Anton. I knew, for sure, that they called each other on a daily basis, probably talked about me but maybe more about themselves. They were getting very close and beginning to act almost like soul mates.

Looking back, I am not quite sure what I was trying to prove, but I was still highly motivated to expand, whatever the cost. The problem was that I had nobody to help me organize and manage so many different places. In reality, Herta and I needed a break, a vacation, where we were both completely alone with each other. Both of us seemed to be going in very different directions and I wanted a vacation that would help us get closer again.

My idea of a vacation differed from Herta's. Where she preferred the beach over everything else, I wanted adventure—anything that remotely resembled my life, that's what I lived and breathed. Spending my time rolling over on a blanket to add a tan to a patch of skin was as remote to me as taking a class on needlepoint.

CHAPTER

# 21

# Lima, Peru

*I tried to ignore the obvious problems and keep
focused on the bright side of Peru.*

I had a favorite uncle, Dr. Ludwig Sitter, my mother's brother,
who lived in Peru. He moved to Lima in 1945, working as a
Catholic priest and missionary until 1960, when he left the
priesthood and became a lecturer at the University of Lima and
professor at the Santo Toribio de Mogrovejo and La Pontificia
Universidad Catolica.

He had been married and named his first born after me and
had a daughter two years later and named her Maria-Agnes.

Although he had visited Austria several times over the years,
no one in our family had ever visited Uncle Ludwig before. That's
where I decided to go on our next vacation!

We always had gotten along well and were quite close.
Whenever he visited, he told me how great Lima was and regaled
me with stories about the strange, ancient city of Machu Picchu

and of Cuzco, the highest town in the Andes, where he had been the leader of the local Catholic Church for fifteen years.

Besides talking about Lima and his work, my uncle also often talked about the jungle and the Amazon. These stories were very exciting to me, especially when he repeated his promise that one day he would bring me a little monkey from the jungle, one so little that I could carry him around in my pocket.

As a child, I was excited for years about my forthcoming pet, but that day never actually came. I always wondered if I went there, would I possibly see the little monkey I had coveted so much in my childhood?

When I thought about his tales, I had to smile. There I was, a small child, standing before my uncle with big, saucer eyes, my ears flooded with his golden words, and with my mouth wide with astonishment at his amazing stories.

Uncle Ludwig told my parents many times that they should let me go to Peru. He promised that I could study there and he would teach me Spanish. He swore this would bring me powerful benefits in the future, but my parents never would allow it. I had to work in the restaurant along with my brother.

Although I was enthusiastic, Herta wasn't. It took time to convince her to consider a vacation in Peru. Finally, she agreed and we booked our round-trip flight and hotel for three weeks.

We arrived in Lima in July and soon found ourselves in the midst of a huge welcoming party that my uncle had thrown for us. All of his friends and my aunt's relatives were there, and we had fun through the night until early the following morning.

It was the first time I had met my aunt and my cousins, Maria-Agnes and Hansi. Everybody was really sweet and overwhelmed us with their hospitality. My uncle had a fine house and he did everything imaginable to please us.

Cousin Hansi was only 15 years old, but he already could legally drive a car. He and his sister went to an expensive private Swiss school, Del Pestalozzi, where they learned German and English. Later on, when he was older, Hansi would study at the Universidad del Pacifico.

I was surprised that I got along so easily with him and really loved my little namesake. It was almost like he was a miniature version of me. Hansi had a good sense of humor, but was restless, like me. He loved a little action.

And Lima, I was impressed but at that time, there were a lot of problems in the country: it had a failed economic program; a great many natural disasters; a serious decline in commodity prices; and soaring inflation that had led to civil unrest. To make matters worse, the so-called Shining Path and the growing Tupac Amaru Revolutionary Movement (MRTA) created havoc and anarchy in certain parts of the country-—being kidnapped and ransomed was always a possibility. Further, drug trafficking was on the rise owing to an increasing demand worldwide for Coca leaves.

While we were there, it was obvious that Peru was experiencing an economic crisis, compounded by its government's insistence on borrowing heavily from other countries. The conflict between the Shining Path and MRTA led to a growing government counter-insurgency with human rights violations on every side. Often, Herta and I saw a heavily armed military presence on the streets while we were innocently sightseeing.

I didn't care about all that. In fact, I found it kind of exciting, but Herta was scared to death. Not a day went by when she didn't ask me why the hell we came there in the first place.

Lima was the fifth largest city in Latin America, the majestic capital and largest city in the troubled country. Situated in the valleys of three rivers, the Chillón, Rímac and Lurín, Lima lies smack on the coast, overlooking the Pacific. Called the "City of Kings," it was discovered by the Spanish conquistador, Francisco Pizarro, in 1535, becoming the capital of the new Republic of Peru after the Peruvian War of Independence.

Despite the turmoil in the country, Uncle Ludwig persisted in trying to show us the good side of Peru. We drove around a great deal as tourists, drinking in its beauty: the historic landmarks, the special restaurants, and the enchanting scenery. There was no doubt, Lima, stripped of the problems of the moment, was a wonderful and beautiful city.

My uncle also had a beach house, and to Herta's delight, we were able to spend time on the beach. My aunt was a doctor and he was professor, so they were solidly upper class. But privileged though they were, they had to deal with a very high rate of inflation.

TO LIVE THERE, YOU HAD TO ACCEPT THAT ALL AROUND YOU THERE WERE VERY DESPERATE PEOPLE.

You could recognize the troubled times by little everyday things. For instance, whenever we parked somewhere, Uncle Ludwig and little Hansi would remove the windshield blades from the car and take the car radio with them.

They told me that if they did not remove them, the blades would not be there when they returned. Poor people would steal anything they could. To live there, you had to accept that all around you there were very desperate people: political agitators, rebels, poverty-stricken families, homeless people, kidnappers and thieves.

Considering everything, I tried to ignore the obvious problems and keep focused on the bright side of Peru. Obviously, my Uncle Ludwig and his family did as well, partly out of necessity, but also because they actually loved the country.

The family's willingness to adjust to the turmoil around them and their efforts to make us comfortable only amplified Herta's constant complaining. All she could talk about was how dirty and ugly the streets were, the terrible slums, and her constant fear for our safety. Although I sympathized with her, having dragged her here in the first place, I finally had enough of her negativity.

"Herta, I'm going to ask you to please shut up. You don't realize how ignorant you are; how much you are creating your own unhappiness."

"Creating my own unhappiness, Hans? Look around you! Did I make these people poor? Did I kidnap people in the middle of the night? Did I put machine guns in the hands of the police?"

"No, you didn't. But we are here now."

"I don't want to be here now. I want to go home."

"I know that, Herta, and we will in a couple of weeks. It's impractical to go before that. Besides, I want to get as much as I can out of our visit."

"What can you possibly get out of this place, Hans?"

"For one thing, Herta, I am seeing how safe and secure we have been all our lives. We didn't feel the impact of World War II directly. We have a lovely home, a warm family and lots of friends. I think this experience should make us grateful for who we are and what we have."

"I am grateful. That's why I want to leave. And I want to leave now. I'd rather be grateful at home ..."

I sighed and decided to leave it alone. At some point in your life, you make a decision about whether the cup is half empty or half full. Sometimes when the cup seems the emptiest, it is just a prelude to a full, overflowing barrage of goodness. This is summarized in that useful phrase, *sometimes it is the darkest just before the dawn.*

That was my philosophy—how I chose to look at life. It was a combination of my experience and my faith. Later on, teachers like Tony Robbins would help me to refine what I thought about reality and how to cope with my decision to be a happy adventurer through life, rather than being a passive victim of circumstance.

Herta, who still hugged the stability of a conventional life, was far from making that leap. She had made the choice to not look at life in a positive way, and I finally had the wisdom, for the moment, to see that she could not.

# CHAPTER
## 22

# Cuzco and Machu Picchu

*Today, it is still a miracle—how the Incas could build
such a city so high in the mountains.*

We booked a trip to Cuzco, the historical capital of the Incas, a city perched 11,000 feet above sea level.

The plan was to use Cuzco as the launching pad for our exploration. Once we were there, Uncle Ludwig, Hansi, Herta and myself would take a train and a bus a day later and explore the legendary ruins of Machu Picchu. After that, we would head out to the Amazon and the rain forest.

When we arrived in Cuzco at an interesting trail to start our exploration, the guide explained that we needed to walk very slowly and obey the rules of the journey. These rules included not eating anything heavy and avoiding any alcoholic drink. If we did not comply, we would get altitude sickness.

When I heard all that, I just laughed and said to myself, not me!

When we visited a restaurant before we set off, we were told to drink some Coca tea, again to protect us from getting ill.

Again, I laughed and started with a beer, and finished by washing an enormous meal down with two glasses of wine.

Just before we left, I was given a little package with two pills to combat any altitude sickness that might occur.

"Sir," one of the officials said, "please make sure you have the pills handy, in case you need them."

I said," Thanks," but thought, *They really overdo everything here—probably to impress the tourists.*

We then left to visit a couple of historic places in Cuzco. And along the way, we crossed the marketplace. To my amazement, I found a game room there—in the highest town in the Andes.

Amazed by the strangeness of this, I stepped inside to take a look and was surprised to find the slot machines were from the Austrian company, Novo Matic, where I always bought my slot machines! This seemed an odd place for a game room. And why did someone contact an Austrian company for these slots?

As we moved through Cuzco, we began to climb higher and before us loomed an ancient Inca temple. About that time, I became very dizzy and had to sit down on a large rock. I simply could not find my breath. To make matters worse, I suddenly became noxious. Realizing that I might be experiencing altitude sickness, I reached into my jacket for that little package of pills I got in the restaurant, but my hands were shaking so hard, I dropped the package on the ground.

For the first time in my life, I cried for help. My wife and relatives were quite a few yards ahead of me when they finally heard me. When they

WHY DO YOU ALWAYS HAVE TO PLAY COWBOY?

turned to look, they saw me white-faced and shaking, panting like crazy.

The sun was shining and the sites along the trail were truly fascinating. But suddenly my entire consciousness was consumed with one of the strangest, most terrifying experiences of my life. I swear to God; it was like I was going to die any minute. Although I should have known better, I was shocked out my mind by the suddenness of it all.

*Why the fuck do you never listen to anyone?* I said to myself. *Why do you always have to play cowboy?*

Hell, I was truly miserable. It my own fault for not listening!

Herta opened the packet for me, and put two pills in my mouth. I barely was able to hold the water bottle to my mouth to down the pills. I don't know how long I sat there waiting to recover. My interest in the extraordinary environment faded completely. It was a dark moment.

About thirty minutes later, the medication began to work and I finally started to feel better. I waited, sitting on that rock and not moving, hoping to feel better, until everyone came back. We then went together to the hotel, where we were to stay overnight,

That time, when we had dinner, I was listening carefully to what the waiter recommended to eat and drink. No longer was I acting stupidly. My cowboy attitude was gone and when I thought about it, I felt like a "fucking asshole."

Machu Picchu lay hidden from the outside world for such a long time because its location is so remote—almost inaccessible. It is situated 8,000 feet above sea level on a mountain ridge above the Urubamba Valley, 50 miles northwest of Cuzco, through which the Urubamba River flows. Often referred to as "The Lost

City of the Incas," Machu Picchu is one of the most familiar symbols of the Inca Empire, built in the classical Inca style, with polished dry-stone walls. Its primary buildings are known as the Intihuatana, the Temple of the Sun, and the Room of the Three Windows.

The Incas started building it around AD 1430 and was abandoned as an official site for the Inca rulers a hundred years later at the time of the Spanish conquest of the Inca Empire. Although known locally, it was largely unknown to the outside world before being brought to international attention in 1911 by Hiram Bingham, an American historian. Today, it is still a miracle—how the Incas could build such a city so high in the mountains. The nearest town is Aguas Caliente, located only a couple of miles from Machu Picchu, in the valley by the Vilcanota River.

We took the train from Cuzco to Aguas Caliente, the last station before having to take a bus to Machu Picchu. The train ride itself is unforgettable, passing through extensive areas of terracing dotted with the ruins of Inca fortresses.

Emerging from a short tunnel, a series of beautiful agricultural terraces mark the ruins of Qente. In this fertile microclimate, fed by a nearby waterfall, giant hummingbirds are a common sight in the early morning, and you can see bright flowers blooming. At just a mile away from the Inca remains, the train arrived at the town of Machu Picchu. It is surrounded by high, green mountains that cradle the famous lost city, and a myriad of other Inca remains.

Tourists disembark at Machu Picchu to begin their unique experience at the Inca citadel.

IT WAS LIKE A MOVIE DEPICTING THE EXODUS FROM A WAR ZONE.

It took the bus about 20 minutes to climb the narrow, steep, zigzagging dirt track that connects the town and the ancient ruins, sitting majestically at the top of a mountain. Tramping around the ruins was an unbelievable experience—like time-travelling thousands of years into the past. It seemed somehow alive, as if you are connecting with the living past. The footprints of the ancients seem truly alive compared to other ancient places I have visited. That's the best way I can explain it.

We left the ruins of Machu Picchu around 3 PM and by 6 PM, we'd be on our train, heading back to Cuzco. We waited a long time at the train station. As it was finally drawing near, we noticed something really odd. We had reserved seats—we paid for "First Class" seats—but the train was so crowded that there didn't appear to be any seats left at all. It didn't appear there was any way to even board the train!

It was like a movie depicting the exodus from a war zone. As the train approached us, you could see Indians literally hanging out the windows. It was a miracle that no one fell. It was so congested, not only by the people aboard but also by chickens, pigs, goats, and other animals that were also passengers. I could not believe it; there were even people sitting on the roof of the train.

The train whistle blew a couple of times, but the train never stopped. It sailed by and all we could do was watch with open mouths.

Ludwig went into the station and, quite upset, told the clerk that we had first class reservations, paid in advance. The clerk just shrugged and told him that there was nothing he could do. Another train would come later; we should all stop complaining and just wait. It was quite clear that the clerk had no concern for our problem.

It started to get cold and then got colder! We were 8,000 feet above sea level and I was sure, when the sun went down, it would get close to the freezing point. We stood there, waiting and shivering with some two hundred other tourists who had also been abandoned by the last train.

We had to wait an hour before we saw another train. But it was a transport train for farm products, not a passenger train. It blew its whistle, and it also looked like it would not stop. But it did reduce its speed and that provided the opportunity for our tourist guide to bravely jump on the tracks to make sure the train stopped. He had guts, but he could have gotten killed.

What seemed to be an extreme act of courage on our behalf by the tourist guide, it did nothing but inflame the train's engineer, who screamed in Spanish at the guide, "I have no place for tourists. "This is not a passenger train—look!" And he pointed to cars loaded down with fruits and vegetables.

Now yelling, "I'm going to leave, you idiot! If you stand on the tracks any longer, I'm going to have you arrested."

But the tourists were more afraid of dying in the cold at the foot of Machu Picchu than being handled by the police. And I thought: *Where the fuck do you think you will find police officers at the end of the world!*

"Why don't you arrest us all!" one of the tourists yelled and made a mad rush with the others to board the train.

Almost instantly, there was an angry crowd pressing on the sides of the train. Some cold, yet deft fingers were prying open the huge sliding doors on the side of each car. Furious and scared people practically climbed on top of each other to get in as fast as they could.

HERTA GLARED AT ME; SHE DIDN'T FIND ANY OF THIS FUNNY.

Herta, Uncle Ludwig, Hansi and I managed to open a car full of oranges. Pulling each other in quickly, we climbed on top of them. Other tourists scrambled aboard, and inadvertently created a giant fruit press. With fifty people piled on top of these fresh oranges, it was no wonder that juice was flowing freely out of the sides of the train car.

It would have been laughable if we were not, at this point, half frozen to death. I wondered what other kind of fruit or vegetable juices were flowing from the other cars.

As the pandemonium reached new heights, so did the voice of the engineer, whose angry shrieks blended with the cries of chickens, dogs and angry tourists. And, as much as he may have hated it, the engineer now had to drive a passenger train to Cuzco, a passenger train somehow loaded with a lot of smashed fruits and vegetables.

When we settled down and began to look around at the crazy scene, I started to giggle a bit. Herta glared at me; she didn't find any of this funny.

Seeing her pique in this ridiculous circumstance seemed somehow even funnier than just being a human orange juice squeezer, and my giggles turned to chortles. Uncle Ludwig, who was also squatting on a mattress of wet fruit about five feet away, infected by my laughter, started to laugh quite loudly. This made

Herta even more annoyed, and her petulant response to our laughter and the growing snickering of the people around us tickled my funny bone. Instead of a few trickles of laughter coming out of me along with the orange juice, I started to snort with laughter, culminating with huge belly laughs that infected everyone riding on this absurd, giant fruit punch ball, rattling down the tracks in the middle of a freezing Peruvian night beneath lofty, ancient mountains. Herta proceeded to lecture me, and I slowly transitioned into a more somber mood. Meanwhile, we and the other passengers huddled together for warmth, stinking of sweat and orange juice, until the errant train rumbled into the Cuzco station almost precisely at midnight.

CHAPTER

## 23

# The Rain Forest

*This was the kind of adventure you could never
have back home ...*

Despite Herta's continual complaints, the next day our little party was on its way to the Amazon River and the rain forest jungle. Our target was the city of Iquitos.

The only way to access that city is by air or by boat. From Iquitos, our boat soon reached the Amazon River and headed to the Yarapa River, its remote tributary. And from Iquitos, there are no roads leading into the jungle. The only way in is by boat.

Finally, we arrived at our lodge, settled in and then made our first excursion into the rain forest. Even in the lodge, we could not forget the jungle—its sounds were everywhere. The entire visit was amazing.

The rooms of the lodge were quite open, only divided from each other with a four-foot-high wall. An outhouse was our bathroom and the shower was a huge funnel, where the rain water was collected. You can bet that Herta was freaking out completely.

As with the train, I got first-class rooms—yet another joke on me! I can imagine what the travel agency guy was thinking—what a stupid idiot, asking for first-class tickets in the Amazon—only a fool would do that! However, he was smart enough to charge me at least double when I requested them.

The next day we awoke to lovely sounds of the morning birds. When I opened my eyes, the first thing I saw were two Blue Crown Conure Parrots sitting on an armrest and watching us. Herta and I were amazed at their friendly audacity.

After breakfast, we made yet another excursion into the rain forest, exploring three pristine lakes, homes for a wonderful variety of birds, primates and pink dolphins.

I finally saw the little monkeys my uncle had told me about during my childhood when he visited. They were a little bigger than I remembered from his stories, but I smiled when I first saw them and thought about the deep impression those stories had made on me.

We were hiking in the afternoon in the jungle, when my cowboy mentality surfaced again when I spotted a tree lying across a river. Of course, it presented an irresistible challenge. I just *had* to try to cross the river while balancing on that tree. And yes, I slipped and fell in.

Immediately, I thought piranhas would devour me in seconds so I swam like crazy to get to the river's edge. Everyone in the party now realized what I had tried to do and unsympathetically shook their heads.

I THOUGHT PIRANHAS WOULD DEVOUR ME IN SECONDS SO I SWAM LIKE CRAZY TO GET TO THE RIVER'S EDGE.

I was completely soaked and we returned to the lodge. Herta commented, "You will do anything to get a little attention, won't you?"

"I guess so." I was quite embarrassed by the foolish accident. Still, I was glad not to be fish food.

We then went out in a small boat to explore the jungle at night. Again, we heard first-hand the thrilling jungle sounds, and watched alligators swimming right beside our boat. We soon found a blink of light from our flashlight would frighten these huge monsters, and they would disappear into the depths of the Amazon.

This was the kind of adventure you could never have back home. In my catalog of personal memories, it was exciting and unforgettable.

As we returned to the camp at night, the moon caused beautiful fluffy clouds to glow between a rich, dark blanket of gleaming stars. It was as though the night rolled out the perfect setting for romance and, for the first time in many years, Herta and I began to talk about ourselves, our separate worlds, and our hopes for the future. We sat comfortably at a long wooden table, gazing at each other in the light of the silver moon overhead. It had all the settings of a perfect evening.

For the first time in such a long time, we talked peaceably with no fighting. Still at the end of this rare conversation, I again recognized the extreme difference between her world and mine and our hopes and dreams for the life that lay before us.

She told me frankly that she wished I was more like Anton and would spend more time at home, like a family man. She said this somewhat bravely, I thought, considering how well she knew me and my adventuresome, entrepreneurial compulsions.

I unintentionally shut her up when I pointed out that Anton was spending more time with us than with his own family.

After that exchange, we became quiet and just listened to the strangely beautiful music made by hundreds of insects, wild beasts and night birds, creatures who came alive beneath a giant, silver moon. We watched and listened quietly together, sipping on a rapidly dwindling bottle of red wine.

At some point, I excused myself and headed toward the outhouse, which was half-hidden in the shadows behind the lodge. When I was finished, I opened the door and found myself looking straight into the eyes of some jungle creature!

If I had not just finished my business, I am sure I would have soiled my pants such was my surprise, intensified by a primitive, naked fear. Whatever the thing was—I thought it might be some kind of bear because it was big and dark—it was not in the least bit frightened of me.

Either he had already eaten or thought of me as too poor a specimen to bother with, and so stumbled back into the jungle without a backward glance. I thought, neither bears nor piranhas had lucked out that day—maybe I wasn't their dish. And no, I said nothing to Herta upon returning to the table. If she had heard about my bathroom adventure, nothing on earth would have kept her outside that evening. I was glad not to have her frightened and freaking out, because our lovemaking was very intense that night. Perhaps she had become entranced by the magic and music of the jungle.

In the morning, I told one of the staff members about my encounter with the strange beast. After hearing my description of the "bear" creature, he laughed and told me that it was a harmless Coatimundi that always hung around the campsite. It was a big animal, and despite its long snout and long tail, it did have a little bit of bear in its facial features.

The next day was our last day in the rain forest. That day would be memorable, largely because of a long hike and a visit to an authentic Indian village, buried in the jungle, where I again felt like I had flashed back to 1,000 years ago.

The Indians of the village were naked or barely covered with nose rings and big earrings and scars and tattoos on every part of their bodies. The tribe showed us how they fished and hunted with blow guns, then the local shaman explained how medicinal plants were harvested in the rain forest. The night concluded with a traditional tribal ceremony before our long walk back to the lodge. It was our last night in the jungle.

Back in Lima, we spent the last week sightseeing between long spells of relaxation and casual dining. Miraculously, Herta and I slowly became close again and the magic of love ignited again in our hearts, a flame almost dampened to extinction by so many years of emotional separation.

We began to pay attention to each other, and hugged and kissed more often. These were precious moments, as if our love had blossomed again.

Then the last day came and we had to leave. With our luggage full of souvenirs, I prayed that customs would let us keep them.

And taking leave of my uncle and his family was not easy. Everyone accompanied us to the airport. We all had tears in our eyes and we promised to return.

After that emotional farewell, there were obstacles ahead of us.

Customs separated us after we checked in. They put me in a room and made me take off all my clothes. I asked them why, but the customs lady harshly told me to shut my mouth or they would throw me in prison. It was a strange way to treat visitors who spent money in their country and had not demonstrated the slightest trace of criminality during our stay. Two military men with machine guns stood beside me, amplifying the seriousness of her threat.

> THANK GOD, I HAD THE GOOD SENSE TO BE TICKED OFF IN MY MIND ONLY.

It was easy to surmise that my personal inspection team was looking for drugs. I shut up and endured a prolonged look in my mouth, and a less than gingerly investigation of my behind and a meticulous search of all my clothes.

I began, toward the end of this inspection, to be really pissed off. We should have been warned! Thank God, I had the good sense to be ticked off in my mind only.

When I was finally finished I thought, "Oh my God, what would they have done to Herta?"

I wasn't really finished with my thought as she came out from a room where they had searched her and the first thing she said was, "Really, really that's happened to me!

"That's the last time I am going with you on your adventure trips. The people here are animals and crazy."

They were not friendly at all, imprinting in my mind the only completely negative happening in Peru. The alligators, Coatimundi bears and piranhas were frightening, but they didn't behave like complete assholes.

We finally made it to the airplane and were on our way back to Vienna.

CHAPTER
24

# Anton Again ... and Romania ...
# an Invitation

*The Communist government famously bugged every
room, and tapped the phones as well as every
pay phone within a half mile.*

After our vacation in Peru, Herta's life and mine began to unwind to where we were before we left.

I began to feel the effect of so much financial risk-taking in the midst of growing responsibility to carefully handle so many businesses and so many employees.

Anton Duda came back in our lives again. The recurring pattern of weekends with Anton started all over again: tennis on Friday; then a swim and a sauna at our house; a patrol of various business sites; and dinner in a nice restaurant, culminating with a stop at one of our discos.

Eventually I got so good at tennis that I started to beat him. At that point, I discovered an unexpected side to my wife's best

EVEN WHEN WE WERE ALONE, SOMEHOW OR OTHER, HE WOULD MAKE AN APPEARANCE.

friend. When he lost, Anton would lose all control, cursing me and calling me every foul name even I could think of. He simply, categorically, did not like to lose, ever.

He found excuse after excuse for why I won unfairly: I played too defensively; I lobbed the ball too much; or I tricked him by not giving him an opening to "really hit" the ball. Anton's Achilles heel was his desire to win at any cost. His excuses for losing were laughable.

Finally, I had enough of his bullshit and told him that I was no longer interested in playing with him. In less than a day, Herta replaced me as Anton's tennis partner.

As one month after the other flew by, Anton would come regularly to my office. Strangely, he would use my phone to call my wife and sometimes talk to her for hours. It didn't really bother me; I just saw them as good friends.

I did think it kind of strange how much time they spent on the phone. I also heard a couple of comments from friends of mine about Anton's omnipresence when we were together. Even when we were alone, somehow or other, he would make an appearance.

I was not actually jealous of Anton. All through my life, I never believed you can force someone to love you. However, I made a commitment never to allow myself to be interested in a friend's fiancée or wife or any of my female friends.

For me this was an unbreakable law. In my mind, I guess I expected all my friends to have the same rules as I did. Hence, my lenient attitude toward Anton's relationship with Herta.

## A Side Adventure Begins

Business seemed okay and I was making money.

On a regular basis, Karl Andritz also visited me at my car lot, sometimes to bring me some car parts, but also to have lunch and spend time with me. I really loved Karli. He was a bright spot in my life. One day, he asked me to fly with him to Bucharest in Romania.

He would be visiting a huge agriculture exhibition and thought we could make some useful connections there if we went. He had been there before, while selling auto parts for his company, and had already established some meaningful contacts with new clients and prospective buyers.

Karl told me how astoundingly poor so many of the people were, and how amazingly pretty the girls were. So, whenever he went to Romania, he brought a truckload of lipsticks and panty-hose for the ladies, as well a few select designer jeans.

"Look, Hans," he said, "maybe you can rack up some new customers for your cars, but whatever happens, I think you will find it quite interesting and we'll have some fun—for sure."

In 1984, Romania was still in the Eastern Bloc and had put up a lot of restrictions on doing business there. Nicolae Ceausescu was President and ruled that country somewhat eccentrically—an understatement. He had a strange cult following that responded to his increasing interest in nationalism, resulting in the deterioration of foreign relations with both the West and the Soviet Union. Nevertheless, owing to the city's elegant architecture and the sophistication of its elite, Bucharest was nicknamed "Little Paris of the East," sharing a Parisian ambiance with Beirut in the Middle East.

⌒

When Ceausescu invested huge amounts of money borrowed from Western credit institutions to modernize Romania in the 1980s, he forced his people to go on a rigorous austerity program to pay for his grand conceptions. The idea was to repay the foreign debts as soon as possible, even at the cost of radically downsizing his people's standard of living.

The standards of living plunged considerably as Romania exported most of its food and fuel production. The population was severely controlled by the secret police, called the "Securitate," and the government, dominated by the Ceausescu family, squandered much of the nation's remaining wealth on megalomaniac constructions and feasts.

FROM OUR FIRST STEP OFF THE PLANE, WE FELT WE WERE BEING WATCHED.

All those years, the Ceausescu regime slowly dragged the Romanians into an economic deadlock. His regime was dominated by lies, corruption, terror, violation of human rights, and isolation from the Western world. The country was full of spies and secret undercover police to protect and defend the corrupt regime of Ceausescu. It was a screwed up situation—nobody trusted anybody. The politicians at the top had everything and the rest of the population was poor and starving. It was also hard to explain that to Americans who had never seen empty warehouses and food markets. It was hard to believe—there was nothing available. The shelves in the department stores and grocery stores were empty.

When we arrived at the Bucharest airport we were separated while customs agents searched our luggage, immediately finding the ten pantyhose, gobs of lipstick and jeans we had squirreled away for the destination. The only chance to deal with customs in those rough days was to give them a taste of your contraband. Karli understood the logistics of all this, and we managed to pass through without incident, and some of the customs agents walked away with lipsticks and pantyhose for their girlfriends.

From our first step off the plane, we felt we were being watched. We quickly grabbed a taxi, a black Volga sedan, and headed to the Athenee Palace Hotel.

During my entire visit, I felt like I was a main character in a James Bond movie and in just a moment or two James Bond would come around the corner and introduce himself.

Besides being a place of intrigue, Bucharest has a large share of historic charm. We passed through the streets of the old City Centre, stared with awe at the grand architecture of the old Royal Palace and were taken by the lush green foliage of Cismigiu Park.

As we drove through the city, I made a note that one day I would make a point to explore all the museums and art galleries and perhaps visit some of its quaint orthodox churches.

Along the way to the hotel, the taxi driver barraged us with questions. During the "friendly" inquisition, Karli looked at me in a funny way, meaning this guy was probably part of their Securitate.

The city was beautiful. But, for a modern, ought-to-be-bustling city, there was surprisingly little traffic.

Karli pointed out that most of the automobiles on the street were either Volgas or Ladas, produced in Russia. When I began to look for myself, I saw this was true, but then I noticed a Mercedes.

"As far as I can tell," Karli said, "those types of cars are generally driven by some politician or a member of Ceausescu's own family."

Communism in Romania was like everywhere else, an excuse to develop an economic elite with special privileges under a repressive dictatorship that controlled the flow of high level goods and services to that elite while the rest of the population scrambled just to survive.

THAT HOTEL BEAT WITH THE HEART OF BUCHAREST, GEOGRAPHICALLY, ARTISTICALLY, INTELLECTUALLY, POLITICALLY— AND, IN A MANNER OF SPEAKING, SPIRITUALLY AND MORALLY.

The Athenee Palace Hotel was in the heart of Bucharest on Episcopiei Street. It was a location straight out of James Bond or the Bourne Supremacy film franchise. You could call it a hotel. But you could also call it Spy Central.

Athenee, as a setting, literally dripped luxury. Gold gleamed from the crevices in its marble pillars, on its great glittering chandeliers, its ornate picture frames and around the edges of its large mirrors, and richly coating the bulky sculptured ornamentation of its walnut bureaus and tables. Men, mostly men, sat half-buried in black leather armchairs in deep settees placed well back in the recesses of the lounge, whispering to each other with half-smiles and furrowed brows. Was all this chattering about trade, political machinations, financial bonanzas hidden in this strange bastion of communism and cultic nationalism, or was it, perhaps, questions about us, visitors to this lost country submerged in the shadows of secret intrigue?

True to the ambiance of the hotel, the level of comfort and service was very high at the Athenee, but was deployed by a very corrupt staff, always seeking to exchange their customer's money at black-market rates. The inflation of their own currency was huge and the best way to pay was with dollars.

Among all this intrigue, the Athenee Palace Hotel had another level of unsavoriness. It was also known by international travelers as the site of a fierce competition by beautiful, local Romanian ladies of easy to nonexistent virtue to share the warmth of a client's bed.

That hotel beat with the heart of Bucharest, geographically, artistically, intellectually, politically—and, in a manner of speaking, spiritually and morally.

Karli told me he had been warned by his business partners, and his friends in Bucharest told him about the nature of the Athenee—so he was careful and prepared. It had both its advantages and disadvantages for doing business.

He told me the hotel director was a retired undercover colonel, now working for the Securitate. The doorman did surveillance, and the housekeeping staff photographed all documents in the guests' rooms. The prostitutes were allowed to roam the lobby, the bar, and the nightclub doing business, but they had to report directly to management.

The Communist government was having fun with that hotel. It famously bugged every room, and tapped the phones as well as every pay phone within a half mile. Moreover, the entire hotel was staffed with informers. This was no secret to most of the guests who sat in the settees chatting up their schemes. It was just the cost of doing business for the opportunities latent in Communist Romania, despite the inconvenience. Nonetheless, everyone in the know understood they had to be very careful, because the Ceausescu government did not mind putting its visitors in jail for conspiracy or spying on the government.

For tourists Bucharest was a hard place to find decent food and sufficient alcohol. It was Ceausescu's playground for special visitors, but a trap for the careless participant in a "casino" filled with the house's own loaded dice.

As a frequent traveler, I was only moderately impressed by the luxurious trappings of the Athenee, but extremely impressed by the outrageous and almost universal attractiveness of its women.

The women were consistently beautiful but also very poorly dressed in inexpensive stretch skirts and blouses. These women were like Vogue models dressed in rags and doused in cheap perfume. I now knew why Karli insisted on the pantyhose, lipstick and jeans.

When we got out of the cab, Karli warned me very explicitly as to how I should behave in the hotel. "Look, Hans, whatever you do, don't say one fucking word about business or our connections here. I'm not kidding. And definitely, don't make a single joke about the regime or about Communists either, as funny as this place is going to seem to you during the next few days."

He went on to say, "Think twice, my friend, before you say one word. If ever you have something important to tell me or you have some kind of pressing question, we will have to leave the hotel and take a walk. Everything we do or say is being monitored."

Karli looked at me intently as he warned me. In all the time I had known him, he had never spoken to me like this. It was because he had carefully studied this strange environment for some time and had decided it was worth it to chance the risks inherent in the situation to do business, but he wasn't going to lose his life—or mine—over it.

"Please don't forget what I'm telling you," he warned.

"I won't. I promise." What else could I say? Karli seemed worried as hell.

# CHAPTER
## 25

# An Angel in the Night

*"Yes," I said, "but what kind of drink are we mixing,*
*a love potion or a Molotov cocktail?"*

It was 5:00 PM when we finally arrived at the Athenee. We took two different rooms, as prearranged by Karli, and agreed to meet in an hour in the hotel bar. We could talk over drinks while listening to live music. It was like I was transported to a different world, one with new, unpleasant rules. It was my first visit to the Eastern Bloc, an experience both strange and fascinating.

I came ten minutes early and ordered a Manhattan that had already become my standard drink when I visited a bar. It was a classic drink, called by some "a man's cocktail"—strong, urbane and simple. When I ordered it, the bartender asked if I had any special instructions, since Manhattan drinkers were often scrupulous about their favorite drink.

I told him my recipe for the perfect Manhattan was two ounces of bourbon, a half an ounce of sweet and dry vermouth and two to three dashes of Angostura bitters. He listened carefully, then mixed the drink.

"Stir it, please," I said, "but do not shake it. Serve it straight up with a lemon twist and two cherries." As I sipped on it, I began to really feel like James Bond, although Bond's signature drink was a martini.

This was my signature drink, and I was sipping it in the middle of a strange but scintillating hotbed of intrigue, just like Bond, surrounded by spies and security police.

I lost myself in my James Bond fantasy, reliving some of my favorite scenes with Sean Connery, who, despite his replacements, will always be my favorite James Bond actor.

From that moment, as I built my own cinematic detective fantasy, I then knew that the Manhattan would be my trademark. James had his martini and a PPK Walther; I would have my Manhattan and a 38 Smith and Wesson Colt.

> WHEN YOU CAN DREAM IT, YOU CAN ACHIEVE IT!

I began to smile about my childish thoughts, but really, isn't anything possible? If I could actually sit in this strange environment and survive, could I not also write about it? Could I not also create a character like James Bond, Ellery Queen, Mike Hammer or Phillip Marlowe? Could I not produce films like that or play the part?

Heady stuff for someone directly in the sights of surveillance cameras and a tangled web of real secret police and real black marketers, but somehow as readily capable of becoming a reality as anything else. A sentence from Walt Disney came to my mind: *When you can dream it, you can achieve it!*

I decided to relive this appetizing little fantasy again on some other occasion—just as Karli walked in. I was lucky to have this experience, however dangerous and scary. I really loved my life and the strange places my business brought me. It was a thrilling life, a life without boredom, a life at Full Throttle. Wow!

> SHE LOOKED LIKE EROS INCARNATED, TOO PERFECT TO BE TRUE, HER GORGEOUS BODY IMMERSED IN THE ACCELERATING RHYTHMS OF THE DANCE.

Karli sat down and ordered a drink for himself. Tonight we would have dinner and then visit a nightclub.

Tomorrow, he said, we will meet a very nice guy, probably the only half way meaningful thing he said in the bar. The rest of the time, he seemed to be saying petty and ridiculous things, a show, perhaps, for the surveillance cameras. What we said had none of the meaningful quality of even our most trivial banter. But outside of us, who would know that?

We then headed to the restaurant, where we ordered Beluga caviar—the only place this gourmet item was available in Bucharest. We washed it down with a bottle of Krimsekt, then took our waitress' advice for the main dish and spent the rest of the time talking nonsense, but somewhat funnier than before. I think we were getting into the act and loving the idea of being on stage, even in a public restaurant.

I couldn't help feeling that everybody in the restaurant was staring at us. But what the hell, we were having a ball!

After dinner, we went to the nightclub and listened to some great, live Greek music, a type of music that I truly love. We then ordered another bottle of Krimsekt and I fell into a trance, listening to the fabulous music.

A few minutes later, I awoke from my reveries by some visitors to our table, two very pretty and well-educated girls. They introduced themselves as Natascha and Ricola. They began the conversation in English, but as soon as they recognized we spoke German, they switched to German. From the very first moment, Ricola paid complete attention to me, while Natascha very obviously concentrated on Karli.

After a few drinks, we moved to the dance floor. Soon enough, I found myself dancing Sirtaki, the dance popularized by Anthony Quinn in his cinematic role as Zorba the Greek.

In Sirtaki, participants dance in a circle, putting their hands on their neighbors' shoulders. The dance starts slow, but gets faster and faster, soon featuring dynamic hops and leaps by the dancers.

I danced with Ricola for what seemed an endless period of time. The dance was arduous and I began to sweat profusely, though completely transfixed from the rhythm, music and alcohol.

I danced my brains away that night.

Ricola danced beside me. She, too, was sweating, her shoulder length, curly black hair swinging to the rhythm from the Sirtaki, her dark brown eyes shining in the kaleidoscope light of the dance floor.

She looked like Eros incarnated, too perfect to be true, her gorgeous body immersed in the accelerating rhythms of the dance. I had the feeling I was in a different world, an erotic planet, too sensual and exciting to be true.

When the band took a break, we panted over to the bar and ordered two vodkas, which we both drank with one big gulp. Two other rounds followed, consumed with the same dehydrated gusto.

I looked around for Karli, but he was gone.

As I slumped down at the table, Ricola bent over me and whispered, "Can I come with you to your room, please?"

"This is not a good idea." And then added, "I'm married."

"You know, Hans, you only have today. Today is really the only thing we have. If you ditch me now, I will definitely get in trouble. Do you understand?"

I looked at her. So much was going on inside me. She was certainly beautiful, but she was also, pure and simple, a desperate Romanian woman ... and a call girl ... and maybe a paid spy.

"After all this time, they will think I have lost my edge and I am costing them money."

Here we go! I thought and I sighed. Perhaps what she said was true, but so what? I had other things on my mind. Admittedly, though, one was her gorgeous body and sweet, respectful manner.

"Believe me, job or not, I would want to be with you tonight. Can't you feel the rapport, the chemistry between us?"

"Yes," I said, "but what kind of drink are we mixing, a love potion or a Molotov cocktail?"

"It's not about money. I want to be with you tonight," she said, somewhat insincerely.

At least the insincere part was what I thought. *Damn, what should I do?* She was not just Eros incarnate, she was pure *sin* incarnate.

On her own, Ricola ordered two shots of vodka. We downed them as quickly as before but not because of dehydration—rather the excitement building between us. Suddenly she embraced me. I sensed her tongue lightly caressing my ear.

She was a strange mixture of illusion and reality. I could smell her cheap perfume, but I could also feel her perfect skin. We looked in each other's eyes and seconds later we explosively kissed, our bodies glued to each other in sudden, riveting passion.

I don't know how we ended up in my hotel room, but she was standing naked in front of me, offering her perfect body, passionately, excitedly. It was like a dream.

Soon we were both embracing, hugging each other as we knocked over a table and rammed into a chair, falling on the floor—it was one of the wildest erotic adventures of my life. Everything was instinctive; we were lost in our pleasure. After a time, I passed out.

I woke up in the morning to a disturbing, relentless banging on my door. Looking around for Ricola, it was clear she had left. And, I was conscious of having a terrible hangover.  I tried very hard to remember what happened last night as I stumbled to the door.

When I opened it, Karli was standing there, smiling. His first words were, "You okay, buddy?"

I didn't really know what to say. I was really thankful for the previous night and my experience with Ricola. Yet, I felt like shit when I thought about myself. Deep inside, I had two feelings, gratitude for my lustful adventure ... and guilt over my infidelity.

Karli and I were good friends and knew each other's wives. I really did not know what I should do. Should I tell him and put him in a position to lie for me?

But Karli was smarter than I was, and quickly said, "Whatever. I really don't want to know anything about last night." Speaking softly, still smiling, "It's your deal. It's already 9:00 AM. We have an appointment at 11. I'll wait for you in the breakfast area but hurry up!"

I felt totally fulfilled by my little adventure, and saddened by it, but that was not perfectly correct.

In the middle of the night, while Ricola was still sleeping, I woke up and checked my pants for my money. Beautiful or not, I was a bit leery about call girls who were notorious for stealing things. Were my wallet, my money and passport still there? Nothing was missing and I felt like a real asshole. I really should listen to my heart, and when I was honest to myself, I had the feeling she really enjoyed being with me, and in that moment she wouldn't give a shit about money.

I also thought of the image that girls like Ricola have and how greatly she is judged in that image. Most people would call her a "whore," but from my perspective, I judged her as a princess, somewhat fallen from her throne. Owing to her circumstances, she was badly treated and forced to act as a spy. A poor life for any young woman. I believed she had a good heart.

After thinking about her, I knew this adventure would be stored forever in my mind. She will always be an angel—an angel who gave me an unforgettable time.

That was the first time I cheated on my wife. I had plenty of opportunities, but I hadn't wanted to hurt her. Although I recognized that our sex life was not the greatest any more—everything was kind of routine, but not bad at all. Still, I felt the growing distance between us. It was 1984 now and I had been with Herta for 13 years!

At that point, I began to search in my mind for some excuse, some justification for my behavior. A somewhat routine sex life was probably not enough. Then, for the first time, I thought about Anton.

After all, I said to myself, somewhat hypocritically, because it had never even remotely bothered me before, *Aha! Who knows what she's doing with Anton? Maybe somehow this is really bothering me, not on the surface, but somewhere deep inside.* This sounded great, but the truth was, despite all appearances, I had never thought they were having a sexual relationship. I looked at Herta's feelings about Anton as a kind of misplaced hero worship, based on his job and security and his appearance as a culturally sophisticated intellectual.

But I had seen how he handled losing in tennis, and I no longer looked at him as so urbane and sophisticated. I sort of liked him, and maybe he needed a friend, too. After all, how much was I around for Herta? The truth was: it was very close to "never."

To the rest of the world, particularly considering certain of my friends' comments on the situation, which I completely ignored, Herta's relationship with Anton was dicey at best. There were even friends of mine who, in trying to clue me in, implied that there was gossip that the three of us were a ménage à trios, something that I would consider to be unhealthy at best and probably quite immoral.

But I was too obsessed with my own life and business to be worried about gossip. Let's say, in general, I regarded Anton as an overly committed babysitter who, in some ironic way, looked at me as a successful role model.

Why did I think so? He had told me as much. He envied my lifestyle, my freedom, and my entrepreneurial adventures. What he had that I didn't have, apparently, was the time to hang around people socially.

CHAPTER

# 26

# Back to Business

*If you want to do any business here at all,*
*you have to drink a hell of a lot of vodka.*

I now headed to breakfast, focusing on the events to unfold today and how I could best help my friend, Karli.

When I got there, Karli was in a hurry. We ate breakfast quickly and then went in the front of the hotel and waved for a taxi. This time we nailed a black Lada 1700i. Not much of a surprise for a street sparsely populated with cars and trucks from Russia—and little more.

Karli shouted out a few instructions to the driver and then we sat back to enjoy our ride. As we drove through the wide and handsome Bucharest boulevards, we passed the Arch of Triumph. God, it did look like Paris! The only difference was the absence of traffic.

We arrived at the agricultural exhibition, the original purpose of our journey. Ninety percent of the exhibitors were from the

Eastern Bloc. The rest were from the West, more of them than I had expected. Germany was heavily represented, followed by France, Italy and Spain.

We went inside the huge convention center, looked around a bit, and soon Karli walked us to a huge warehouse in the middle of the exhibition. We entered and climbed up a narrow staircase, leading to the second floor. Karli knew exactly where he was going.

We found ourselves in a little office with air so filled with pungent cigarette smoke you could almost cut it with a knife. As soon as we entered, this huge guy jumped up, looking more like a nightclub bouncer than a manager of a company.

His name was Vladimir Voda and he was the director of Bucharest Import/Export. Smiling broadly, he hugged Karli enthusiastically and in a loud, deep voice exclaimed, "Dowarisch, Karli, my friend! What's going on?" He then lifted him like a feather. I could hear Karli gasp as all the air left his lungs, so powerfully had this monster of a man pressed him to his chest.

When he put Karli down, I had to marvel at his size. Karli was big, 6'2", but looked like a midget next to Vladimir. I fantasized that we had just encountered a distant cousin to Rasputin.

After he had finished happily greeting Karli by crushing the air out of him, he turned to me. In my case, thankfully, he only shook my hand enthusiastically with his huge, bear-like paw. At one point, I thought he would break my fingers, but I managed to survive the welcoming ceremony.

His joyous, gargantuan gestures demonstrated how excited he was to see both of us. He then smiled and roared, "Vodka, please!"

An attractive woman—maybe in her forties—quite well-proportioned, her blond hair tied in a ponytail, stepped into the room with a bottle of vodka. Introducing herself as

ALWAYS GULP IT ALL DOWN. IF NOT, YOU RISK INSULTING YOUR HOST.

Nanuschka, she quickly passed some whisky glasses around while Vladimir the Monster filled them half full of vodka. He then roared again, "Nastravje," and gulped his glass down.

Karli looked at me and said, "You know, this was the main reason I went to bed early last night—to be able handle my vodka in the morning. If you want to do any business here at all, you have to drink a hell of a lot of vodka. If you don't, you will run the risk of offending a prospect."

He looked at me as Vladimir smiled complacently at both of us. "Always gulp it all down. If not, you risk insulting your host. There, that's your first Eastern Bloc secret of success."

I don't know how many times we lifted our glass and bellowed out "Nastravje," but it was a lot. We wound up drinking to the health of his whole family, and, as I remember, he had a very large family, and so did we.

Finally, we went to another room and met some other guys. I cannot remember everybody's name, but Vladimir introduced us to everyone.

The first thing Vladimir said was a kind of security alert. "Okay, Karli," he said, "we can finally talk. I made sure that this room is not bugged—like everything else is. And I guess you know, you have to be really careful about talking about anything on the phone, particularly business."

The first thing Vladimir did was to order some engine parts from Rothmund, Karli's company in Vienna. Then, suddenly, other deals were put on the table. One of Vladimir's friends—associates—specialized in metals. He told us they could deliver Zirconium and Tantalum from Russia to Vienna.

These metals were known to be both highly resistant to corrosion and have a very high melting point. They were used frequently in missiles and space rockets as well as other specialties.

Soon, other stuff was put on the table. I really can't remember it all, possibly because of all the rounds of vodka that went around during this somewhat frenzied conversation. I do remember that everyone insisted that this would be only the beginning, and that we would all be good friends from then on—that we would make something special happen and we would all stay in touch. I tried to talk about my used cars, but no one seemed to be paying that much attention to specifics at that point.

After meeting Vladimir's friends, we went around to a few other companies at the exhibition, but at that point—it was early afternoon—I was pretty much plastered. We made a lot of contacts, though. The future would prove how useful they would turn out to be. We definitely had one hell of a collection of Eastern Bloc business cards.

I WAS TIRED AND FELT THE MULTI-HOUR DIP IN THE COLD VODKA SAUNA WE HAD JUST IMMERSED IN.

After all that business drama, we took a taxi back to the hotel, thinking we would rest for a few minutes. But Karli had second thoughts. He wanted to stay in the cab. "I have to see some of my former customers in Bucharest," he said. "I think they want to re-order. Anyway, I promised them, so I might as well split now."

"You don't mind if I hang out here," I said, obviously wiped out from all that drinking.

"No, of course not. If I don't see you tonight, it's probably because I took Vladimir out for a good time. I'll wake you in the morning. We have to leave by 9:00 AM to make it to the airport in time."

"Hey, be careful! I'll see you soon! Thanks for everything," I said, jumping out in front of the hotel. I walked briskly inside, and headed straight to the elevator and to my room.

I was tired and felt the multi-hour dip in the cold vodka sauna we had just immersed in. Man, I was sorry for Karli. They might have to pump vodka out of his lungs as he was sure to almost drown in it if he sealed a couple more business deals by the end of the day. To be sure, his vodka immersion was not yet finished.

After years of knowing Karli, I thought of him as a real friend and a great guy to hang out with. But so far, this had been our most outlandish adventure.

I took off my clothes and fell in the bed. By the time I woke, it was dark outside. I looked at my Rolex and it was already 9:00. I checked for the symptoms of the outrageous hangover I should have had. Outside of a rumbling in my stomach, signifying an impending attack of voracious hunger, I had no other symptoms. I didn't even suffer a headache.

I took a quick shower, put on a fresh shirt and pants and was soon on my way to the bar. The bartender was the same man who mixed me my first Manhattan in Bucharest. This time he told me to call him Igor.

I ordered my Manhattan and Igor repeated my instructions to the letter. "Stirred but not shaken, straight up with a twist of lemon and two cherries," he said.

"Absolutely," I said.

When Igor gave me the manhattan, he batted his eyes and coyly asked, "What do you think about Ricola?"

By now, I was accustomed to this strange place's indulgence in continual and unrelenting spying on everyone within earshot. So I wasn't altogether surprised by Igor's question. I got it; everybody knew she was with me that night.

I told him that she was a "great lady" and I really appreciated her company.

Igor said he liked her, too, that she had a very good heart. And, did I know that she was going to the University and planning to be a doctor? "Wow, good for her!" I said, a little surprised at the loftiness of her plans.

I finished my Manhattan and walked to the restaurant for dinner. After dinner, I went for my last visit to the nightclub. There was no Greek party that evening, just a guy at the piano bar playing songs a la Frank Sinatra and Dean Martin.

The songs were nice, but there wasn't anything near the magic of the night before. I sat there for about fifteen minutes when someone touched me lightly on my shoulder. Seconds later, I felt a kiss on my cheek and a tongue in my ear.

I turned and looked straight in Ricola's eyes. She smiled, kissed me on my lips and said, "I'm glad you're still here."

I replied softly, "I'm glad too, to see you again, baby."

She sat down and I ordered a bottle of Krimsekt and Beluga Caviar to get a little something in my stomach—I had enough hard drinks for one day. We were both very calm and relaxed; it seemed like I was talking to someone I had known for years.

She told me a sad story of personal survival and her need to take care of her aged mother. Her father had died recently in an accident and she needed her job to finish her education.

We talked for hours without stopping. We told each other our stories. For me, it was a very special exchange, delivered in soft voices

HERTA AND HOME WERE FAR FROM MY THOUGHTS.

because of the harsh reality of Big Brother's relentless desire to soak up every private moment of his captives and finally, we got up and went to my room.

That evening was, again, a lover's dream. It is impossible for me to describe the beauty and subtlety, but I can say that our incessant lovemaking was punctuated with some sleep. Herta and home were far from my thoughts, but somehow, I felt a vague discomfort in the background of my mind, a kind of disappointment in myself, despite the ecstasies occurring within the four walls.

A loud knocking woke me up in the morning.

I looked around and Ricola was still here. I looked at her and her beautiful naked body and gave her a kiss on her forehead, then jumped up opening the door only a crack, because I still was naked. Through the crack, I saw Karli. He just stood there, smiling, saying nothing.

"Okay, I will be ready in 10 minutes," I said. "Is that okay?"

"Take your time. There is no hurry. I'll see you downstairs for breakfast. And, as far as what you did last night, it is not a problem for me. I see the problem you have with your wife and your friend, Anton. I'm not here to judge you, one way or the other."

He was right. It was a burden to wonder what he thought of me. And it was a relief that I could sit alone in my own room, trying to figure things out, without worrying about someone else.

Ricola was up already and in the shower. I joined her and we made love again under the hot shower. It was amazing, but soon it was over and on its way to be another picture in my inventory of memories.

We put on our clothes and I went to my luggage to pull out all the pantyhose, lipsticks and jeans I had. Then, I got my wallet and gave her 200 dollars. She had tears in her eyes and said, "Please don't think bad about me. Please remember me in a positive way."

"Yes, baby, I will. I will remember you as an angel, and that's what I believe you really are. Keep your goals in your mind and one day I hope to hear that you are a doctor."

She looked very sad. "Who knows? Maybe we will see each other again," I added.

I believe that this would have sincerely pleased both of us, but I also knew that would be a miracle. So, we remained silent.

Then I said, "You know, you can have breakfast with us." I took her hand and tried to leave with her.

She shook her head, "No, Hans, I don't want to." I think she didn't want to make our good-byes too painful. But whatever the reason, I kissed her a few times and she was finally persuaded to come to our final meal in Bucharest.

I was happy to bring her and not have to disguise anything in front of Karli. We were happily laughing and chatting together as though we were just a normal, happy couple in the middle of Romanian Spy Central. I noticed, in these circumstances, no matter how ecstatic and happy I was with Ricola, that I felt the eyes of the world on us. Were there people in the back rooms of this hotel, recording and taking notes on every nuance of our conversation ... of what we had done in my room?

After breakfast, I kissed her good-bye as a Volga Estate pulled up to take us to the airport. Riding in the car, I became lost in thought, brooding on everything that had happened in this strange, unpleasant world.

When we finally took off, I told Karli everything that had happened and everything in my mind. In keeping with that vital rapport I had with him, I recognized we were now more than good friends. I had the feeling I found a brother and sad to say, feelings I had never really experienced with Franz, my real brother.

# 27

# Preparing for the Future

*I thought, fucking bastards. What kind of a state*
*provides this kind of alternative for its people?*

I saw the world a little bit differently when I returned from Bucharest. For one thing, I thought a lot about communism, not as a theory, but as a reality.

Romania was not a system of government where wealth was shared in some equitable way. It was a kind of dynastic, totalitarian government in which the dictator and his cohorts, including his family, received the fruits of the average person's labor, a labor enforced by a brutal secret police that had no regard for human freedom or the rights of the ordinary man to have any kind of opportunity in his life.

As someone who has lived in a form of democratic socialism, I do have a respect for people's entitlement to education and medical assistance, but I have also seen a danger in that system when it represses innovation and entrepreneurship by over taxation and giving government far too much regulatory power over the minutia of business operations and expansion.

Communism, as I saw it in Romania, far outstripped any kind of moderate socialism that provided real benefits for the people of Austria or other Western nations.

In fact, it was kind of a farce, because it wasn't real socialism at all. Democratic socialism means government that empowers people to survive, grow, be educated and be healthy, but there is also a component of its policy that allows individuals to innovate and grow their own businesses, if that is their choice. Whereas Austria may have restricted real entrepreneurship, Romania had strangled it, forced it underground and created a slave state in order to maintain its dictatorial control over people's bodies and their minds.

The Soviet-sponsored communism of the time, in all its variations, created suffering and starvation for most of its people except for a few assholes that ruled the country with an iron hand, those who followed them in some kind of official Party elite and special friends, family and trading partners of the ruling class. In my mind, Ceausescu was not one bit better then Hitler. He ruled with terror and fear and killed everybody who rejected his iron will.

I thought a lot about Ricola, how smart and pretty she was, and what a beautiful time we had those two days. Defying most of the stereotypes one might think about call girls, she spoke four languages fluently and was planning on becoming a doctor. Still, I remembered how thankful and happy she was when I gave her the pantyhose and the lipsticks. I remembered her reaction when I gave her $200. At first she cried, then had whispered thank you in my ear, while cautioning me not say anything aloud. Was this because Big Brother was listening and maybe they would take this money away from her? An amount of $200 was two full months of living expenses there, much more than an evening of frivolity.

I was sorry that Ricola had to work as a spy and call girl to survive in order to have the opportunity to finish her education and earn a real living in a decent way.

Believe me, I heard many stories from call girls and why they had to do what they did, but Ricola didn't present herself in this way. She told me what she did and she didn't apologize for it.

Given the circumstances and the fact that a pretty girl in Romania was very likely to be targeted as a pawn of the power structure, it is quite possible that her career was offered to her with the alternative being jail or death. I didn't know and I really didn't want to know.

The communism of Romania, in fact all the configurations of the Soviet Bloc, was basically a dictatorship of the few over the many, engineered by a giant propaganda mechanism to convince as many citizens as possible that their government was one of both law and virtue, while a secret police functioned inevitably to make sure that those who did not buy this ridiculous nonsense would still conform to the state or wind up in jail or a Gulag. I thought, *fucking bastards. What kind of a state provides this kind of alternative for its people?*

After Ricola, I was forced to examine myself, thinking a lot about my marriage with Herta. I still loved her, but if I was honest with myself, it was more like the feeling for a good friend, not on the level of desire and love that you should have for your own wife.

I saw her parents and her life. Day after day, year after year, it was the same. At 7 AM you leave your home; at 5 PM you come home; at 6 PM you have dinner; at 8 PM you watch TV; and at 10 PM you go to bed.

Then, there was their damn vacation. For 30 years, they went every single year to the same place in Caorle, Italy—the same little hotel by the sea. When I asked them why they went to the same place every time, the answer was always the same, "We know what we get and what we can expect." Oh, my God! All my mind could scream was ... *boring!*

I knew this would never be the kind of life I wanted. Just thinking about it shocked me. When I tried to paint a picture of our future together in this scenario, I was filled with terror.

Herta was a problem. Should I tell her what had happened in Bucharest? How could I do that to someone I supposedly loved? And, if I did, no matter in what way, would it not hurt her to the core?

Every year we would spend a couple of days discussing the possibility of children. From her point of view, she had enough of kids in school, but if I would change my life, then she would think about it.

I had a couple of major problems with this. First, I didn't want to change my life at all. I liked my life! And secondly, I did not want my children raised according to the lifestyle suggested by my in-laws, who would certainly have a hand in raising them.

Would anyone want their kid to be told by your wife's parents, "Look, your father is an egotistical megalomaniac who only cares about business and nothing about you or your mother. Don't listen to him."

I am not exaggerating. That is what they would do, with the full cooperation of Herta and other family members. As a dad, I would be walking around in my house with a permanent black eye.

Thinking about raising children under those conditions drove me half insane. For me, the decision to have children was serious, deadly serious. I believed a child had a right to loving parents, a mom *and* a dad, not a couple headed toward divorce a few years later, with the grandparents lying in wait to actually raise the child because of the exigencies of single parenting. No, I didn't want that to happen to my child!

I was pretty open-minded about other people's lives, but in terms of that issue, in regard to having children in a marriage, I was old-fashioned with no compromises. Perhaps it was not just "old-fashioned," but something deeper. Perhaps it was my "core" values, although I was—and am—hesitant to legislate morality for anyone else.

I compared my experience and adventure with Ricola and the life I was stepping back into with Herta. Certainly, our relationship had become *very peculiar.* For one thing, she talked to Anton ten thousand times more than to me. When we went somewhere, he accompanied us like a little dog.

I don't mean to imply here that I didn't like him. He was quite intelligent, had consistently good manners (except when losing in tennis), and I enjoyed our conversations. In many ways, he was a deep thinker and had profound knowledge of many subjects.

But in regard to our visits with each other, he never brought his wife or anyone else with him. I expected that his marriage was in some kind of trouble because he never stayed at home. Yet, he did not speak badly about her and did talk a lot about his kids, who were eleven and thirteen at the time, but that was it. In a way, despite his omnipresence, he was a man of mystery with mysterious intentions.

If I tried to put myself in Anton's position, deciding to hang with a man and his wife day and night, I would never ever do it. No fucking way! I would have felt like a spare tire. I couldn't fathom why he did it. So why didn't I just give him a "ticket to ride?"

I always thought I could get rid of Anton in five minutes, if I really wanted to.

I did not see him as a romantic competitor, and I actually liked him as a friend. This is the really sad part— perhaps I was actually scared to be

> "YOU CERTAINLY HAVE BITTEN OFF A LOT, HANS."

alone with Herta because, quite honestly, we disagreed in so many areas, and, when we didn't, well, things could be quite boring. So I endured the reality of our uncomfortable threesome and put all my energy and focus into my businesses.

When I came back, nothing had changed, except I knew this running around between businesses was not good for me. I had to find some help to organize and control my little empire or I would freak out permanently. There were too many odds and ends to tie together; too many people to keep in touch with; too many miles to travel to retain some kind of real semblance of management.

During this chaotic time, my brother's wife had a second child and, during a time of extremely high stress because of my failure to find an assistant, the event actually gave me a much needed break. The newborn was named Florian, and his birth

was an opportunity for our various families to "come together."
We came together all right, but nothing had really changed.

THE MORE MONEY
I MADE, THE MORE
BUSINESSES I OWNED,
THE MORE I WAS
COUNTED AS "ROGUE."

Everybody asked me how things
were going, and when I explained, they
would gasp, not in admiration, but in
fear, saying stupid things as before like,
"Oh my God, I hope this works out"
and "You certainly have bitten off a lot,
Hans."

On the other hand, I also had to hear my relatives heaping
praise on Franz. Now he had two sons, Martin and Florian; he
worked for a government school; and was actually stable and
prosperous, unlike me.

Despite my lavish and conspicuous lifestyle or the number
of businesses I owned, they didn't count for anything in their
stability-worshipping minds. Money earned through any kind of
risk was clearly taboo and could only have been engineered
through someone lost in his egotistical megalomania and entrepreneurial fantasies.

My reaction was to try to provoke them as much as possible
and to delight in their upside-down reactions to real success.
So I told my stories—watched the unyielding solemnity and
stupidity of their reactions—and counted myself happy.

As far as I was concerned, I would rather die a thousand
deaths than change places with any of them.

I'm afraid, if I secretly wanted a better image with my family,
my conspicuous disdain for their conventionality changed me
from a kind of maverick entrepreneur—harmless but a little
crazy—into an actual black sheep of the family.

But this was because I was in an Alice-in-the-Looking-Glass world, not the real one. So these people, with their upside-down thinking, turned my successes into some kind of kaleidoscope of failure. The more money I made, the more businesses I owned, the more I was counted as "rogue."

When I left for home, and the grueling routines I had built for myself to manage my businesses, I honestly had tried to find a director and controller for my restaurants in Theresienfeld and Vienna and, with Siegi, two game rooms, two Café Harlequins, three dance clubs, three other restaurants, five Beer Mugs, and one gas station.

These were twelve distinct businesses and, although everything was finely tuned to my mobile needs, my eccentricities and comfort, slowly but surely I became overwhelmed. I needed that help badly. Still, despite the many applications I received, I was slow to choose my new managers.

Finally, I chose Peter Pelts who worked for a restaurant chain in Austria called Wienerwald. He soon began working and I prayed to God that he would take a lot of the workload and pressure off my back.

His main job was to drive from one place to the other, to take inventory, to control and organize bulk purchases, and to position us in every way to enhance our profitability and control our overall expenses.

I soon hired another person just to handle the slot machines. That person brought the cash to me every day, allowing me to keep absolute control over the cash flow. The result was that on the slot machine side of my business, I eliminated all possibility of cheating and made a very good profit from the gambling proceeds.

The restaurants, discos and Beer Mugs worked perfectly with the slot machines; the slots bringing steady and reliable profits. But, without gambling, every single one would probably be losing money.

I allowed myself to be hypnotized by my success with the slots and ignored the problems with the restaurants. I also did not pay sufficient attention to the car business, where the number of trade-ins had reduced profitability and created an increasingly difficult-to-manage inventory.

Looking back, I think it was largely a matter of psychological burnout.

In the car business, it is not a good idea to make your actual profit in trade-ins that sit there, unsold, on a parking lot. And that's what actually was happening—there was a stock of 150 cars and growing.

Yes, the cars themselves might have been valued at one million dollars, but all they did was stand around and force me to pay "interest" on their cost of storage and maintenance.

Yes, I hired managers to help me. But I didn't show them how to settle the profitability issues with the car and restaurant business issues, and manage them back into the black.

Instead, I focused on my prime personal issue—the relationship with Herta—and expanding into yet another new business, which I shall explain shortly.

I tried to salvage my relationship with Herta. Perhaps because of guilt and perhaps because I still had a spark of hope left in me, I tried to work on my relationship with her. I carefully began to monitor my treatment of her, being consciously nice to her whenever possible. But, when the weekends came, it was the same story. Anton was always with us.

When I tried to protest, she immediately jumped to his defense, saying how lonely she was when she went to the discos and I had to talk to my managers and guests—how she needed him for entertainment. Wasn't he funny and smart? Didn't I enjoy his company?

Well, needing an antidote to Anton, I started to invite Karli and his wife, Annemarie, and Annemarie's sister and brother-in-law to our sauna evenings on Fridays after tennis.

It was interesting to see how Anton and Herta reacted to this new situation. They didn't say anything, but they were both obviously unhappy! While Karli and the others, myself included, were laughing, drinking, jumping in the pool and having real fun, Anton and Herta acted increasingly reserved. They hardly smiled at all.

I liked it though, thinking I had found the right medicine to take a break from our problematical threesome.

On Saturdays, Herta and I often went to a restaurant called Taubenkogel, or The Pigeon Bin in English. The Pigeon Bin was located in Schuetzen, in Burgenland, three miles from Oslip, where I ran my parents' restaurant.

There, Walter and Evelyn Eselboeck had created a unique gourmet restaurant. Walter was a completely self-taught chef and Evelyn was perfect and charming in serving the guests. I often wondered why my wife could not be a little more like Evelyn.

Walter was unbelievably creative in the kitchen and both had a real passion for their restaurant. I liked them very much.

Often we stayed awhile after dinner, sharing a bottle of wine with Evelyn and Walter at our table. Soon, we became good friends. As you may guess, most of the time, Anton was with us.

Over time, Walter became a Grand Chef and received two Michelin stars. At one point, Wolfgang Puck himself came to the restaurant and they cooked a special weekend menu together.

CHAPTER

# 28

# Anniversary

*I was ready for the new challenge—ready for another major adrenalin rush.*

When I had a family event, normally I booked it at the Pigeon Bin and it was always a great experience.

During this period at my attempt to be more attentive and close, Herta and I had an anniversary. By this time, I was determined to improve our relationship and I looked very hard for a very special present.

Remembering some of our good times in the Peruvian jungle, I bought a Scarlet Macaw parrot that cost me $3,000 along with a huge cage to go with it. The pet store owner told me that he could also be placed outside but his wings would have to be clipped so he couldn't fly away.

I put him in the indoor swimming pool, creating an atmosphere with an exotic touch without letting anyone know of my gift for her.

That bird was huge, almost 36 inches high; his tail was magnificent.

When I bought it, the store owner told me it was not easy to get a parrot like that because it was against the law to import Scarlets since the breed was rapidly becoming extinct.

The birds themselves, he said, are very intelligent, much more so than most birds, but they need a lot of attention. When they are ignored and not stimulated, they get very demanding, even aggressive.

I made a reservation at the Pigeon's Bin. While we were having dinner on our anniversary, Karli went to my house, put a tree next to the cage, preparing everything so it would be a perfect surprise for my wife.

Unbelievably, Anton tagged along with us to our anniversary dinner. Herta seemed so excited about his presence, that I did nothing to stop it—I wanted to please her and didn't want to start the evening out with a cloud surrounding us. Anton apparently had a present for our anniversary.

When we arrived, Walter and Evelyn happily hugged and kissed us, but then Walter whispered in my ear, "Have you adopted Anton as a son? I mean, can't he leave you alone on your anniversary?"

"I agree," I whispered back, "but let's forget it for the moment— I want Herta to be happy."

After that brief exchange, the three of us settled down to a great five course menu accompanied by a rich sampling of great wines, especially chosen for us by Evelyn. In fact, each course was accompanied by the perfect glass of wine, which could have made the setting for the ideal, romantic evening if Herta and I had been alone.

Still, despite the awkwardness of Anton's presence, he did add to the festivities of the evening, in a sense, regaling us with his funny stories and banter. If it had been any other night, and if the rude rumors about our alleged ménage à trois weren't disturbing me, I would have enjoyed the evening as an evening out with friends.

Around 11 PM, Walter and Evelyn joined us, opening up a bottle of champagne, giving Herta a beautiful bouquet of roses in an expensive crystal vase as an anniversary present. When we left the Pigeon's Bin, it was already midnight.

Anton had his car parked in front of our house, so I invited him for a last drink and with the idea, of course, to show him the present that I had bought for Herta. But upon entering our indoor swimming pool, the parrot began to hysterically scream, scaring her half to death.

Despite the Herta dramatics, I couldn't help noticing what a great job Karli had done, putting that tree so close to the cage so when it was opened, the parrot could easily climb onto a tree limb. Perched there, staring at us, he would have really added an exotic ambiance to my little swimming hall.

But at this moment, we were not dealing with anything quite so pretty, rather a virulent, angry bird that was carrying on like he was in the middle of a jungle at night, awakened rudely by intrusive predators intent on his destruction.

When she calmed down, realizing there was nothing to fear, she got very excited about her present. She, too, had pleasant memories of our romantic evenings in the jungle and gave me a sudden hug and a kiss.

"Thank you so much," she said. "That parrot is really beautiful and a very special present."

Anton also complimented me on my gift, telling me it was such a rare sight to see in an Austrian household. Herta loved my surprise!

We then turned the lights off in the pool area and went back to our living room. I fixed one drink more and Anton left for the evening. Finally, we were alone.

We took a shower and had a very beautiful, intimate evening I had looked forward to. Still, afterward I thought how the relationship with Anton had somehow spoiled our closeness, and how I had lost any real desire and excitement about our relationship. It was a strange feeling.

## Back to Business

Karli was on my mind the following morning. I called him to thank him for the way he had set up the parrot cage near the pool and arranged the foliage to enhance its new home. Then, I also told him about a guy who owed me some gambling money, and who had a one-acre lot in Neudoerfel, around 10 miles from my car lot. The acre was on the main street of Burgenland and he had offered to give me that property instead of the money.

I decided to take it on the assumption that something was better than nothing and maybe here was an opportunity for Karli and me to work on another deal together. So I asked him if he might consider building a shop there to sell parts from his company, Rothmund's. There was no one in the area with the kind of motor parts his company specialized in and this could be a win-win scenario. It took everyone in the area, including myself, an hour to get to Vienna to buy those types of parts.

As the sales director there, Karli said he would think about it and, if it seemed sensible, he would talk to the owner about it. Maybe he could arrange a kind of joint venture with me.

I WAS CONVINCED THAT KARLI WOULD DO EVERYTHING TO MAKE THAT DEAL WORK.

True to his word, the very next day Karli invited me to meet with him and join Mr. Rothmund over lunch. I wound up in a private room in a posh Viennese restaurant, explaining to him what I had in mind, which was to build the shop and get parts on consignment from Rothmund's.

The margin was 100 percent. That meant, for example, If I bought something for $10 and could sell it for $20, I had enough profit to give a dealership a 30 percent discount and would still make money. I liked the idea. But much more, it inspired me with the idea of working more often with Karli. I liked Karli very much and knew—with his sales and reorganization talent—the company would make money. It would be a much bigger opportunity for him, than sticking with Rothmund for the rest of his life.

We had a long lunch and drew up a plan that was executed in just a few days. Karli would be in charge of our joint venture from Rothmund's side and I would handle my end. Mr. Rothmund was very happy about the deal.

I was excited about my new idea and the business model. For once, not everything was on my shoulders. I was convinced that Karli would do everything to make that deal work and help me find the right employees, and I knew he was perfectly qualified to handle inventory control and sales. And the bonus: we would see each other more often.

When I returned from the meeting, I immediately called Herbert Plangl, a customer of mine who owned a construction company. He had already bought four vehicles from me and I liked him.

The only problem with Herbert was he had an uncontrollable passion to talk about his hunting experiences. When he started to drink, he would launch into an account of his adventures and quickly turn off any non-hunting enthusiasts present. And when people wanted to leave, he would get upset. But he was the kind of a person that would make a deal with just a handshake. His word was gold. He would never try to finagle out of a deal that he had made.

I soon brought Herbert over to the property where I wanted to place the parts shop. In a couple of weeks, he presented me with his plans for constructing the building. I told him that I would contact him in a few days and give him an answer to his proposal. Then, I called Karli and we decided to meet the next day at the Beer Mug on the Opera Ring in Vienna and go over the plans for the store.

The following day, I left earlier than usual for my office, deciding to patrol all my Viennese Beer Mugs. I drove to the First District and it was funny, even though I was very busy as always, today I had a strange but positive feeling.

I left the Autobahn and went on Hwy 17, called Triesterstrasse, where my car lot was located. I passed it and saw all the Mercedes, BMWs, Porsches and the one Ferrari in the front row and suddenly had a singular feeling of pride.

Despite whatever my relatives thought about me, I considered myself, at heart, a true entrepreneur and, to me, that was a good thing. The German word for "entrepreneur" is "unternehmer," which means "to do something, to take challenges, create new things." That's how I thought of myself.

Although my relatives and other people around me attributed my actions to greed, egotism or insanity, and whatever I did would never be enough for me, all that was a misinterpretation of my motivation.

I never was just running after money for its own sake or to inflate my own reputation for the sake of ego. The fact was that I wanted to do things, to accomplish things, to leave my footprints on the world. And I knew working for other people would never accomplish this. Besides, I enjoyed the risk, the ups and downs, the challenges to make things happen— the thrill of the ride!

Yes, I took things to extremes. And, yes, I created stress for myself by taking on so much: like this new project with Karli.

But still, even with all my unresolved management issues, a new business opportunity excited me—a new business plan, a new building, a new staff, a new consumer market. I was aware of all that concern about extremes but I was ready for the new challenge—ready for another major adrenalin rush.

CHAPTER

# 29

# Vienna

*Isn't it amazing that Vienna was the home for Mozart,*
*Schubert, Beethoven and Johann Strauss?*

Despite this new business opportunity, stressful anticipation was not the driving force in my consciousness. On a par with my sense of self-esteem when looking at the prestigious inventory of cars I had laboriously accumulated over the years, I felt a kind of parallel emotion about the world around me as I drove to the First District in Vienna.

Instead of focusing on business, I focused on how beautiful Vienna was that morning. Instead of inventory or business, I began to feel grateful for the beautiful locations of my Viennese businesses, and how lucky I was to enjoy my surroundings.

Vienna is not the largest city, but it is the capital of Austria and considered the cultural capital of the world, with around 1.7 million inhabitants. It has an unbelievably unique charm and flair. Tourists from around the world have made Vienna the most urban tourist destination in Austria. Vienna is to Austria like

Venice is to Italy, a city for anyone who is romantic and for anyone who loves history and music, specifically classic music.

Vienna is also famous for its classic coffee houses and the Heurige, its traditional wine taverns, and for famous culinary specialties. Our kitchens are very special with a great mix of different cultures, habits and customs.

You can probably understand why I loved soaking up the ambiance of these great cities. And as in Venice, and later in Monaco, I would sit in its cafés and wine taverns, speaking to many of their guests and saturating myself with the subtle shadings of the streets and business life of these cultural Meccas.

If you happen to read Hemingway's immortal classic, *A Moveable Feast*, set in Pre-World War II Paris, you can see how coffee houses and taverns function for writers and artists—sometimes the very muse needed to seed their next work.

I don't know the way that genetics functions with geography. But isn't it amazing that Vienna was the home for Mozart, Schubert, Beethoven and Johann Strauss?

I VOWED THEN TO PAY MORE ATTENTION TO THE PROFITABILITY OF THESE RESTAURANTS AND STOP NARROWING MY FOCUS TO THE GAMBLING COMPONENTS.

The arch stereotype for classical music is probably the Blue Danube Waltz, but the reality is that a gigantic segment of Western music's classical heritage comes directly from Austria.

Vienna is an ancient city and the hallmark of the Hapsburg Dynasty, the center of the Austrian-Hungarian Empire. The population in Vienna back then was composed of many foreign nationals: Czechs, Hungarians, Slavics and Serbs from Yugoslavia. But that was two or three generations ago, and their descendants are now Austrian citizens.

Vienna currently has 23 districts. The historical part, the First District, is called Innere Stadt, the site of two of my Beer Mugs. The famous broad boulevard, called the Ringstrasse, surrounds the Innere Stadt.

On route to my Viennese Beer Mug inspection, I passed by many impressive public and private buildings and great and fabulous monuments. I also noted the Town Hall, the Burgtheater, the Parliament, the University, different museums, and the Hofburg.

I don't exactly know what had happened to me, because that day, for the first time, I had transcended the success and egoistic glory of success and was allowing myself to experience a sense of wonder at it all. Waves of gratitude overcame me as I awoke from the daydreams of my humdrum management route and began to really contemplate how blessed I was to be here—the world's cultural capital.

The first Beer Mug location told the entire story of my successful geographic positioning in Vienna right next to the Staats Oper on the Opern Ringstrasse. It was a prime location, one of the key factors in making a business work. I was lucky that day and found a parking lot close to my restaurant, and moments later was inside talking to my manager and Mr. Pelts, my restaurant director, who was visiting at the time.

We discussed a number of potentially lucrative changes and I was convinced that these gentlemen were keeping their focus on my business. I vowed then to pay more attention to the profitability of these restaurants and stop narrowing my focus to the gambling components.

Scared of not being able to locate another parking spot near my second Beer Mug on the Burg Ring, I decided to walk. I wanted to savor my mood and absorb every bit of Vienna I could.

When I arrived, I also marveled at what a good location it was, seated right next to a Tramway station. Our Tram system is a modern marvel and I could have taken it from one Mug to the other.

AS YOUR FRIEND, I TELL YOU, HANSI, GET RID OF HIM.

Once at the second Beer Mug, I drilled the manager on as many details as I could and also asked him how Pelts was doing. The details resembled the issues in the other Vienna location and we discussed some typical minor management problems. Twenty minutes later, I walked back to the first location, where I had promised to meet Karli.

When I arrived, Karli was already there. We had a drink together and I showed him the plans for our parts shop. We made a couple of little corrections, but overall, he liked it. We then had lunch, toasting the success of our new venture. When we were finished, I invited Karli to go with me to the Hotel Sacher, about ten minutes away.

Second to coffee houses, I loved to visit hotels that had history and flair, even if I was just visiting their restaurants, bars or coffee houses. As for the Hotel Sacher, it is a Viennese institution, comparable to St. Stephan's Cathedral with a perfect location near the famous pedestrian zone, the Kaerntner Strasse, in the heart of the city. The Sacher was quite close to the Ringstrasse and the Vienna State Opera, where my Beer Mug was located.

Take a few steps away from Sacher's doorsteps and you will be connected to the most exclusive shopping streets in the city, like Kaerntner Strasse, the Graben and the Kohlmarkt.

It was a cultural and political hub if there ever was one, exactly the kind of place I liked to hang out.

Of course, the Sacher is noted for its authentic Viennese coffee house atmosphere, with the reputation of being a glamorous meeting point for politicians, business people, royal families, and aristocracy from around the world as well as writers and artists. This functionality was formalized in the famous Austrian TV series, "Hello, Hotel Sacher!" that drove its fame to even greater heights.

It is also famous for its specialty of the house, the Sacher Torte chocolate cake, a treat which is still exported throughout the world.

Back in those days, I loved to go in the Hotel Sacher Café, eat a Sacher Torte and have an espresso, a glass of water and a cognac. And I wanted to take my good friend, Karli, with me this time to a somewhat more commodious location for an open discussion than at Bucharest's notorious Athenee Palace Hotel.

While at the Hotel Sacher, we both ordered a cognac and talked about our adventures in Bucharest and the new parts shop. But then Karli put down his glass and looked at me intently.

"You will not be mad at me if I speak to you about the relationship between Herta and Anton?"

"Why I should be mad?" I said. "Friends should be able to speak openly with each other."

"Look, Hansi, I think that over just a few years, we both know we are very good friends and can trust each other. I also know for a fact that even though you can be pretty tough in business with your adversaries, with your friends and family, you have a soft heart."

He looked at me solemnly, as if to overcome any desire I might have to potentially dismiss his point.

"This Anton is hanging with you and Herti day and night. Perhaps he means well. Perhaps he is quite a bit your friend, as well as your wife's. But I tell you, I feel strange about it. I don't think it's good for her or you. As your friend, I tell you, Hansi, get rid of him. Get rid of him, now."

I tried to protest. "You know when I take her with me on my little restaurant and disco tours that I spend most of my time talking to managers. If I don't take her with me, I will hardly see her at all. But if I do take her, she gets bored and he keeps her company."

I didn't want Karli to think that his advice was going unnoticed. "Still, it makes me uncomfortable, too. I know exactly what you mean."

"Okay, at least you recognize it. And if you can accept it without a problem, it is fine with me. But I must say, I have to get this off my chest. I really love you and I felt obligated to tell you. You are a good friend."

"Thanks, Karli," I said, "the same for me." We then ordered two more cognacs and left. It was already about 3:00 PM.

Obviously, Karli's comments stimulated more of my determination to decide how to handle the Herta/Anton relationship, but my thoughts bounced off a steel wall in my mind. I didn't want to hurt either of them, but the relationship was toxic. In a subtle way, Anton was stealing my thunder with Herta and that was wrong. But how to fix it?

I stopped at Herbert Plangl's office on my way home. Karli and I needed to know the price for building the new parts shop. This was my lucky day again because Herbert was there and willing to go over the changes Karli suggested. He said that it was no big deal and would have little impact on the price.

He opened up a bottle of red wine and after talking interminably about his hunting experiences, he started to calculate the price. He set his initial offer at $320,000 and then we began to negotiate.

Although I liked Herbert, he was just as tough a business person as I was, and we went forward and backward with the price, something that could be expected with so much money at stake.

The business talk was still interlaced with hunting adventures and, after two bottles more of wine, the hunting got more dangerous and the animals he shot got bigger and bigger.

It took a few more hours rattling between peerless hunting stories and tough-minded price negotiating for us to agree to a fixed price of $280,000 with seven months to finish. One handshake and the deal was done.

It was Thursday and I drove straight home, really happy about the deal I negotiated with Herbert. A $40,000 savings amounted to a pretty good salary for three hours of solid negotiating, punctuated with a great deal of carousing and listening to hunting bullshit.

At home, my grandfather had a table with a sign on it which said, "Table for Hunters, Fishermen and other Liars." Hell, if I could always knock off $40,000 from a project expense by listening to self-congratulatory macho episodes, it would be okay with me.

But don't ask me to sit at a fire in the woods and hear them all night, either!

I had to smile about the day and was in a good mood, although quite tired. I called Herta on the way and asked if she would like to have a nice dinner in the "Hengl Keller" in Wiener Neustadt. She agreed.

I was surprised! An entire dinner and evening without Anton, followed by a private swim together, a sauna and a relaxing night of love and romance. Wow! I thought, after all that, we still love each other. Maybe if I can work on our relationship more, we can work it out.

A few weeks later, Herbert started construction of the parts shop and we founded a company called "Rothmund & Sitter Motor and Car Parts, Inc." It was already September of 1984. My plan was to open up in the spring of the following year.

Herta's birthday was approaching and I secretly bought her a new Porsche 944, one of Porsche's most successful models. Built on the same platform as the Porsche 924 that she was currently driving, this one had a really beautiful body design, looking a little bit like an Aston Martin. It was silver with black leather seats. A knockout!

I said nothing to her about a birthday celebration, but planned a party with Walter to be held at his restaurant, Taubenkogel. We invited all my relatives, Karli with his wife, Siegi and his girlfriend, and, yes, Anton was coming, too.

Walter made a huge cake, forming a marzipan replica of the Porsche 944 on top.

Siegi helped me take the Porsche over to Walter's restaurant, parking the car in his backyard and hiding it under a large plastic cover.

The event was not only meant to celebrate her birthday, but also to

IT WAS AN EXCITING YEAR. *I WAS ENJOYING THE RIDE.*

help cement the strides I thought I had begun to make in our relationship.

This turned out to be a giant celebration, with gypsies from Budapest playing and singing for us as the forty or so guests sampled a fabulous five-course meal meticulously prepared by Walter and his staff. And Evelyn, who handled the service, was more than great. We all were treated like royalty.

At the end of the meal, Walter served the cake that included a model Porsche on top. Everyone naturally thought the ornament was nice—no one but Walter knew what was to come. After the birthday song, I invited everyone outside.

He had already placed fireworks around the covered Porsche and when the guests started coming outside. One of his friends started to fire them up as we all oohed and awed. They were as rich in color and symmetry as any premium, home New Year's private fireworks display could be.

In the midst of all this excitement, I dramatically yanked the cover off and enjoyed watching my relatives, including my sweet brother, gape at the new car. When she saw it, Herta's own eyes widened and she said, "Oh my God," in an unusually loud and unexpected voice. I was really happy for her and hoped, at that moment, that we would find our way back to each other.

It was 3:00 AM when we left—happy, drunk and exhausted.

Until the end of that year, everything went pretty smoothly and, surprisingly, Peter Pelts did not do a bad job of management, despite my lack of involvement and interest for most of the year.

I felt, at this point, I had somewhat cracked the organizational code I had so desperately needed, and expected in time, a higher degree of profitability in everything I did.

Christmas was coming, and two weeks before, I had a last surprise for Herta. It was a present that I admit was more for myself than for my wife—a Cavalier King Charles Spaniel named Elliot.

Elliot was white, mixed with Blenheim brown. I bought him from a breeder in Zurich when I went to Switzerland with Siegi to see what we could do there with slot machines. That little dog cost me $2,500 but he was very sweet and got along with everyone who came to our home. The breed is known for its easy temperament and handling.

I still had my Rottweiler, Harry, and my German Shepherd, Caesar, but they resided on my car lot and I was glad to be with them when I was there. But I really wanted to have a dog at home, too.

My family at home was getting bigger. We had the parrot, Ruby, and now our new dog, Elliot. It was an exciting year. *I was enjoying the ride.*

CHAPTER

# 30

# Troubles—A Confrontation

*The question became: when, and would*
*they put us in jail?*

Another year passed and I stayed busy. Things between my wife and I remained somewhat unresolved, but overall, I thought a lot better.

But something special happened in February of 1985.

The Tax Service staged a sudden blitzkrieg against all large slot machine vendors with the consequence that many of the owners of these vending companies were put in jail.

The front pages of the newspapers were filled with everyone who was arrested. The tax officials said that the coup had been planned over a long period of time. Ultimately, they staged a huge action with literally hundreds of government officers. The goal was to get everyone specified in the charges at once. The invasion was planned this way with no advance notice, otherwise vendors could destroy any evidence of wrongdoing.

Every large vending company was summarily handed a search warrant, immediately followed by a swarm of agents, shortly followed by massive arrests. It became a huge scandal. A media delight for everyone but us, who were now all labeled "bad guys."

In Austria you had to pay sales tax on *all* the money that was in the slot machines.

Why did this all happen?

To understand it, you have to understand one of the unique aspects of Austrian tax policy regarding slot machines.

The reason for this outrageous action: they believed that no one was paying the right amount of tax. In Austria you had to pay sales tax on *all* the money that was in the slot machines. The sales tax was 20 percent. That means, when you had an income in a game room for example, of 10,000 dollars in the machines, you had to pay on this amount, a 20 percent sales tax, which would be $ 2,000! Now, it was pretty easy for a game room, for example, to make, instead, a gross income of 100,000 dollars. That would mean a gross profit ranging from $20,000 to $30,000 dollars.

Then from that gross, all expenses would be paid: the employees, electricity, rent, etc.

Now do the math:

- $100,000 gross income yields between $20,000 to $30,000 gross profit. From that you would have to pay $20,000 tax as well as all the other expenses mentioned.

- Most machines were paying out 70 to 80 percent, so the sales tax destroyed pretty much everybody's

profit if they were paying the correct amount on
sales tax.

- So, automatically to make money, everybody in that
business made a lot of money without putting it in the
books. The IRS (called by us Finanzamt) knew that for
sure, then it was practically not possible to be honest,
so all of us were guilty. The challenge for the government
was to prove it. But the irony from the entire situation is:
how the hell you can make a law for paying tax when
obvious nobody can pay it?

When the tax revenue office said you now have to pay sales
tax for that income, everyone affected started to fight that ruling
in the courts. All vendors thought this was absolutely not right—
fucked up, in other words.

The vending machine owners are actually selling nothing! It
might be okay to pay on the amount that somebody won, but
from the gross amount that went into the machines?

But our tax revenue office did not consider that possibility
and no judgment was made to change the rule. They did not care.
The rule stood as far as they were concerned.

After shoving all the vendors in jail, they began extensive
interrogations. The game was to promise that, if a vendor fully
confessed, he would be forgiven and his punishment would be
radically reduced.

Most of the owners knew that any confession and explanation of their activities might trigger further incrimination against
others. So they said absolutely nothing—not a peep.

Siegi and I became extremely anxious. We didn't know when
the revenue officers would knock on our door. Worse, we didn't

know even *if* they would come at all. We had no clue, and the uncertainty did not help for a good night's sleep.

In the end, we decided they would come. The question became: *when, and would they put us in jail?*

> "**WHAT DID YOU SAY? ARE YOU THREATENING TO SHOOT ME IN THE SHOULDER?**"

We weren't concerned they would find something suspicious. We both were too smart for that kind of shit, but we also didn't want to sit in jail for fucking nothing and how long we would be in there!

During the first week since the arrests, nothing happened. We went on with our daily routine, but as we made our normal cash-in tour to Eisenstadt, located in the province Burgenland, we had that feeling ... somebody was following us. We were on the way to our café, Harlequin, where there were 14 slot machines.

Entering the café, we started our normal routine of opening the slot machines, removing the cash and resetting the counter mechanisms. Counting the money, we wrote out the appropriate cashier slip for the cash and had the waitress or the manager sign it.

We made sure everything was exactly right and left with the cash, every time putting it into a special briefcase together with the slip. We did it that way so that when our technician picked the briefcase up, we had complete knowledge and control of the money.

And sure enough, as we finished and left the café, two guys left a nearby car, approached us and said, "Mr. Holz; Mr. Sitter?"

I replied, "Is that really a question? I'm sure you guys know exactly who we are."

One of them showed us his badge and as we both guessed, they were tax investigation officers.

Siegi said, "How can we help you?"

One of the guys asked, "What do you have in your briefcase?"

Siegi replied, "The money from our slot machines. Why?"

The guy who looked as though he was in charge said, "We guessed right. That is the reason we are here. Would you be so kind as to go with us back to the café ... and please, don't try to run away; we are armed and would use our weapons. You would not run very far with a hole in your shoulder."

My face flushed then and I angrily replied to him, "What did you say? Are you threatening to shoot me in the shoulder? Come on, go for it! Come on! I'm right here in front of you. But only one thing: I would like to see you actually pull the trigger. So you really have to shoot me in the chest. come on, go for it ...!"

"Calm down, Mr. Sitter, that was only an expression!"

"An expression! What the fuck does that mean? An 'expression' to shoot me in the shoulder? You need help, man. What the fuck is wrong with your guys? Why the hell would we run? I guess you saw one *Miami Vice* movie too many. This is fucking ridiculous. What's your name, sir?"

"My name is Mr. Geyer and I am the officer in charge."

I said "Okay, Mr. Geyer, I would recommend going back, and we open the slot machines. You can examine the counter mechanism, and you will see how much the ingoing money was and what the payout was. Then you can count the money and check the receipt for the cash. When you are finished, you owe us an apology, or I will report you to your boss."

"Slow down, Mr. Sitter. Please change the tone of your voice or you will have to come with us to our office."

I became more and more furious and answered, "What the hell is wrong with you, Mr. Geyer? Do you think I am frightened, or would you like to threaten to shoot me again? Maybe you can use another 'expression,' referring to another part of my body! How about this time between my eyes!

"And to go with you to your office! What do you think that threat does to me? What do you think that you can do there? What games do you like to play in your office: good cop, bad cop? Maybe you would like to hit me then, thinking that it helps you to get information. You know what, forget that shit; I have had enough of that already in my life. Anyway, what would you expect then, in your sick mind?

"A great speech from me and an explanation of where we put all our millions. Believe me, I'm too old for your bullshit. I'm not a cheater, and for sure I'm not a fucking rat."

I was ready for a verbal fight, but Siegi pulled me back and said, "Hans, calm down. My parents are still very well known by the director of our revenue service and he is this person's boss. I will give him a call in a couple of minutes. Nobody can treat us like that. Don't worry!"

Mr. Geyer turned to Siegi and said, "Mr. Holz, don't get me wrong. We have to do our job."

Siegi, now angry himself, said, "You're kidding me, right? There is a difference between doing your job and treating us like criminals from the moment you approached and warned us that if we try to run, you are armed. That means you would shoot us, or ...? When you do your job right, you would be nice and polite, first controlling and proving the facts. Anyway, Mr. Geyer, you will hear from us. But, as you have requested—first we are going back to our café and then you can start with your investigation, or your so-called job, whatever that is."

Mr. *Asshole* Geyer said not one word more and went with us back to the café, where we opened up our machines. They started to operate the slots, examine the counter mechanisms, and after that, examine our cashier slips and the money. They could find nothing wrong.

You could really see how much that bothered him. He took the waitress aside and talked to her, and after a time returned and said, "I do apologize, I think I was a little bit tough in the beginning, but you have to understand ..."

I interrupted him and said, "No, I don't understand; forget your apology. You were acting like you were in a wild west movie and not as a tax officer, and anyway, you cannot frighten us at all. You think because your guys arrested a couple of vendors, you can treat everybody like a criminal ... that we will shit in our pants when you guys show up? No way, I promise you that."

His look said more than any words. If he had the opportunity, I felt that piece of shit would shoot me in the back in a heartbeat. He hated my guts, as I did his.

Mr. Geyer said, "Where are the slips from the weeks before. We will come to your office in the next couple of days and pick up all the slips from your different businesses."

Before Siegi could say one word, I spat out, "I cannot wait for that moment. What do you think? How stupid do you think we are? For your information, all our bookkeeping and all our daily records are at our CPA's office.

"I cannot wait until you appear there. I promise you one thing, if you act with him like a tough, wild west cowboy, you will be in jail before I will be."

Again he gave me that hateful look but said not one word more. And the entire time the other guy said not one word. I had the feeling he was not happy with the behavior of his partner.

Finally, they left and Siegi and I went to the bar where I said to our waitress, Gerda, "Give us two fucking Jack and Cokes, and tell me what that asshole was asking you."

Serving us, she said, "He asked how often somebody came to pick up the money and how much it was every time. I told him that it was different every time and we had to sign the slips and count the money. I told him also

> IF SOMETHING HAPPENED WITH THE SLOT MACHINES, IT WOULD BE THE END OF MY BUSINESS.

that most of the time it was not you or Mr. Holz, it was usually a technician—that was all. He also said I should not lie. If I did not tell the truth, they would put me in jail."

I said, "Bullshit; don't worry. That guy is just a big asshole; he can do nothing to you. Good girl. Can you imagine that that motherfucker wanted to scare us. Anyway, we have to be careful. I'm pretty sure it is not over yet."

Siegi and I had a couple more drinks and I gave Gerda a 100-dollar bill as a tip. On our way back to our office, we discussed all of our options. Siegi was in a much better situation than I was. I was fucking scared. If something happened with the slot machines, it would be the end of my businesses.

The car business right now was not profitable. The three Harlequins I had with Siegi made a great profit, but if they shut us down, we would no longer make even one dime. Our game room would be worthless, and I did not like to think about what would happen then. They had no reason to hit us, but who knows what they could invent against us.

# A Big Canary Sings

*You never know what will happen. Someone may
get weak and start to confess ...*

Our best bet right now was to talk to Siegi's dad. We would
hope that he would talk to his friend—the director of the revenue office.

Siegi's dad knew a lot of people with power, but I was very
nervous and so was Siegi.

We did not talk much on our way home, but we did promise
each other that whatever would happen, we would say nothing.
Our bookkeeping was okay and we were certain they would find
nothing. Yet we were still nervous.

After we arrived at our office, I drove home, took a sleeping
pill and went to bed. I did not tell Herta what was going on; it
would only scare her to death.

Siegi called the next morning. His dad had already talked to
a couple of people, and we should be alright, but he heard that

one vendor in jail—a big vendor—was singing like a canary. He had no clue who it was, but he would know in the next couple of days.

I met Siegi at his office and we went to the Airplane Bar where we met with his dad.

"Hi, Hans, what's going on?"

"Hi, Mr. Holz, so far so good. We are anxious and very interested in what you can tell us. You spoke to someone at tax revenue."

"Of course I did. As you know, I have, over the years, my buddies there, and most of them are in pretty high positions. And I have a very good reputation. So far, nothing has happened to your guys, so calm down.

"They arrested at least 10 people from the big vendors and slot machine producers, and they are interrogating them day and night. Most of them have told them nothing, saying, 'Go to hell, I have a bookkeeper and you can audit my company as long as you like.'"

"For sure the tax investigators are trying to scare them with, 'We will see what your attitude is when you are here for a year. It's a long time to stay in jail, so when you tell us everything you know, we will let you go immediately.'

"You never know what will happen. Someone may get weak and start to confess—whatever it may be—but right now, you both are under the radar, so don't worry."

We had a couple of espressos and made small conversation with Siegi's dad for a while and then he left, after which I talked to Siegi about what we should do.

For the next couple of weeks, we agreed to control our slots by ourselves. Nobody else should do it.

A couple of weeks went by and the rumors we heard were that most vendors still had not said one word, and the tax investigators could find nothing so they could prove nothing. But there was also a rumor that one vendor was ready to break down. We weren't sure who it was, but everybody started to get nervous.

> OUR CUSTOMERS WERE SCARED TO GAMBLE WHEN THEY CAME TO THE CAFÉ.

Our normal customers—the main crowd, in fact—were scared to gamble when they came to the café. So our income from the gambling business dropped dramatically, and I started to sweat again.

And when reading the news about the threats, it appeared that our customers might be arrested, too. It was complete bullshit, but we could do nothing about it. The side effect from some stupid article in the newspaper was pretty obvious.

I had a contract with Herbert Plangl who was constructing from the ground up a building for a parts shop, which Karli was to manage and Rothmund would be my partner. By the time it was completely finished, it would be an investment of around $400,000.

Again, I was not worried at all about meeting my payments if everything went smoothly with my slot machines, but if that revenue steam was gone, I would be in deep shit.

Right now there was no money from the car business and all the profit that I made with the slot machines was invested back into my car business, or now, in the new venture, the parts shop.

Three weeks went by since they arrested the 10 guys from the vending business. It was clear now who was talking in jail. We got the news fresh from the jail because we knew an employee there. The big "canary" was Josef Kammer.

In their desperation to extract a confession, the tax revenue officers selected one of the most powerful owners—Josef Kammer— and they sweetened the reward for his confession. If he confessed completely about himself and about all he knew, the agency would work with him in the future and put him in charge of monitoring all the slot machines in Austria. The big canary would become the big fox.

Kammer was very well known in the vending business and to most of us, it was not a savory reputation. He was clearly a threat to everyone else's business.

His game was to target new locations and pay a great deal of up-front money for long-term contracts in game rooms and restaurants. In a short time, he had expanded to a massive 1,600 slots, making him virtually "Slot Emperor of Austria."

If a competitor was already established in a restaurant or game room, he would offer a significantly larger percentage to the owner. Instead of a 50-50 split, he would give the owner 60 percent. He also offered more money for the contract. He used his size as leverage and alienated all the other owners as a result. Basically, he wanted to break everyone else's back in the slot business.

This is a typical anti-Mom-and-Pop business strategy that has leveled small businesses in many industries throughout the world. However, back then, in Austria, all these Austrian slot owners knew each other—and often communicated—so he did this in front of a lot of very offended people who got along with each other and despised his predatory ways.

The price for a slot machine was about $6,000 dollars, so we are talking about serious money. That means his machines alone had a value of more than nine million dollars.

Then you had to add on his office, warehouse, game rooms, the value of the contracts he had developed with game room and restaurant owners, and much more. My guess was, at that time, his company was valued in excess of 20 million dollars.

He grew quickly. Everyone in the industry knew that he wanted to be the biggest vendor in Austria and was making a ton of money.

Kammer was very smart. He also invested every penny that he made back into his company and was on the way to developing his own slot machine, with an original game of his own design.

Initially, the Tax Agency searched his main office, but found nothing to prove he had misreported his sales tax. Still, he wound up in jail, terrified, thinking they had found something, but not knowing what.

The way they got Kammer to talk was simple.

First, they told him he would sit for a couple of years in jail, till the investigation was finished. But then they told him if he would cooperate with them, he would not be punished. All that turned out to be a lie. This part of their strategy was quite typical. Offer them immunity and then they will quack like ducks.

Second, they also promised him they would get him out of jail immediately, another powerful incentive.

These two elements were not unusual. But the third part was an outright monetary bribe.

The result of all this was that he would get back his already powerful company if he would work out some kind of a control system with the revenue officers. The control system would assure that, in the future, cheating by vendors would be dramatically reduced. And in return, Kammer would acquire control over all the cheaters' vending locations.

Considering how the government was feeding his prime motivation, to be the Slot Emperor, they were handing him his throne on a silver platter,

so why shouldn't he be enthusiastic and cooperative?

So Kammer sang ... he told them everything. In fifty or so pages, he detailed every penny he made and how he did it. But, he didn't stop there. He went on to tell the tax agents that he had a second set of books which his secretary had hid in the forest.

Kammer then went with the tax agents to his office and told his employees, "Look guys, thanks for standing up for me so bravely, but I made a deal for us. When we give them all the paperwork, we will get back our company and nothing will be changed. I will be back in a couple of days, and everything will be over."

His secretary went with the agents to the forest and showed them where she had buried the books. And that became the death penalty for Kammer's company.

The idiot gave to the revenue officers, in black and white, the name of every single customer who had ever touched a slot under his name; how much he took; and what the split was. That meant what they really collected and how much they hadn't recorded.

In regard for what the Austrian government promised him, he wrote pages and pages of plans for the coveted control system that the government could use to assure its regulatory authority over the industry.

Within a couple of days, the vulnerable vendor, who had trusted the Tax Agency and prosecutors, managed to destroy himself and his company. The Slot Emperor of Austria went down.

When we found out about Kammer and that he was still languishing in jail, Siegi and I had an emergency conference discussing what we should do.

# A Plan for Survival

*Sometimes you need bad quality shit to make good things grow, so just be a little patient with me.*

The only good part of this was that we never had any business dealings with him. With the latest development, however, we also would now be fucked.

Siegi and I met Kammer a couple of times and neither of us liked him.

How can I explain this? He talked in a low growl, usually about money and in a creepy, persuasive way, especially to prospective clients or when he bragged about his operations. His success wasn't due to his rhetoric, but to the money he had in the bank, and the fact that everyone he approached either knew it or soon would.

Kammer was, in that respect, the real thing. Yes, Kammer had a lot of money. Yet, from the way he personally chose to appear, my guess is that he often slept in his clothes, or at least it looked that way.

He looked like a sleazy, overweight con-artist, who reeked from his bad habits and the greed that emanated from him with his every word.

I remember the day he came into our office with his general manager, Greg Wield, and made Siegi and I an offer to buy our places. We both said, "No Fucking Way!"

Before his association with Kammer, Wield had a sizeable gaming company with about 300 slot machines, two game rooms and one café. So in order to elicit his services, Kammer bought him out for two million dollars and gave him a monthly salary of about $15,000 plus a bonus based on performance. The deal was immensely profitable for both men.

Despite the ludicrous image he presented to the world, and my disgust with some of his actions, I will tell you that as far as vending goes, Josef Kammer was something of a genius, along with being sneaky and street smart.

For me, Kammer was what Americans would call a Damon Runyan character—crazy, eccentric but colorful—in effect, interesting. Siegi actually hated him, so I'd have to pursue a possible deal with Kammer but Siegi's response was, "No! I don't like the son of a bitch, and I don't want anything to do with him."

"Now, Siegi, sometimes you need bad quality shit to make good things grow, so just be a little patient with me."

"I would hardly call that little, fat pig quality anything," Siegi retorted.

"Doesn't he have a lot of money?" I asked.

"Yes, at the moment. But I'll bet it won't be for too long. Look at the poor bastard; he's still in jail. Don't you think, by the end of this, they'll strip him of everything?"

"I don't know about that. But from what I know of Josef, he's probably scared to death now. I know from personal experience; jail is not too much fun.

"**"But do you really want to work with a scum like that?"**

"Yeah, so what? Let him rot in jail for all I care," added Siegi.

I pressed on saying, "There's one good bite in every rotten apple. Sometimes if you're starving, you have to look for it."

"Are we starving?"

"Maybe not you, Siegi, but I am in deep trouble. If something happens with the slot machines ... and, as you know, our income dropped dramatically in the last three weeks. Since that shit happened, it is down more than 80 percent. We are writing, right now, red numbers everywhere. Oh I forgot, I have to add losses from my car business to my red numbers. But if we could get involved in Kammer's business in some way, we could pick up many different places ... and 1,600 slot machines ... with one hit!"

"I guess. But do you really want to work with a scum like that?" questioned Siegi.

"Maybe. Not sure yet. I think I first want to contact his lawyer. See if his lawyer will buy some kind of a deal. And if he does, maybe we can get through to Kammer and see if he will buy it."

"You think there's money in it?"

"I think there's a goddamn fortune in it."

Despite my optimism, Siegi was still disgusted with the idea but offered me some wiggle room saying, "I don't know. But, hell, Hans, if you're so damn sure, make some kind of an approach. Find out something; then we'll see."

AT FIRST SHE LOOKED SCARED.

Accordingly, I went over to Kammer's office and talked to his secretary. As I knew already, his secretary had a brave heart and risked going to jail for her boss, and then that idiot screwed her and himself badly.

There was a disguised purpose to why I wanted to go to his offices. Not only did I want to get his lawyer's phone number, but what I really wanted was to find out as much as I could about his organization—how it ran and the people who worked for him.

When I got there, the receptionist pointed to Kammer's secretary. I could see her sitting at her desk with three other staff members. They didn't really seem busy but were engaged in occasional chitchat.

Being only 9 AM, I headed back out and bought as much espresso and strudel as I could carry and returned to the office. I was asked if I was the new coffee service, but I smiled and said I was a slot vendor here to see Kammer's secretary.

Upon saying that, the others cleared out of the office taking their sweets and drinks with them.

I introduced myself.

"Hi, my name is Hans and news travels fast. I heard you hid the bookkeeping and Josef, that dummy, told you to give records to the tax agents. I don't get it, but I would be glad to have employees like you."

Ingrid was her name and to my delight, quite pretty, and seemed pleased with the strudel. She knew nothing about me but saw me as a possible ally, and seemed happy to discuss the general problem that presently affected her boss and the rest of the industry.

Obviously, she was stressed and worried about her boss being in jail. She seemed to really like Josef, something that really surprised me.

At first she looked scared, but after a while, talking and joking with her, she felt more secure and told me the whole story about the tax agents. And she also began to talk about Josef.

What I found out from our rather long conversation, was that besides owning 1,600 slots and wearing ugly clothes, the little Slot Emperor was actually a fantastically successful boss who won the hearts and very souls of his employees.

How was it possible?

I think it was a combination of his generosity and the fact that he really did not have any personal friends, so he adopted his employees as his friends because they were the only ones he could really talk to and count on.

I am not kidding about their loyalty. It was phenomenal. Not one of them brought him an inch closer to being indicted for tax fraud. Amazing! But everyone in his company was shocked when he told Ingrid she should show them where she buried the books.

Not only were all his employees grilled for hours, but their interrogation was probably more thorough than with any other vendor. Still, none of them—not one—exposed him in any way. And, to be sure, these people were threatened. It was the nature of the prosecutorial game.

And, none of them wanted to do anything but repay Josef for his employment, his generous concern for their welfare and, yes, I guess in some way, his friendship.

Siegi was amazed, too.

Josef Kammer's assets definitely would be his incredibly loyal and competent employees along with having some very smart computer "geeks" working for him. He had been attempting to create his own branded slot machine design with a customized computer program designed by his own workers.

While I was visiting with Ingrid for the first time, I eventually stated my mission: to help Josef with some of the business problems he had accumulated for himself. After my explanation, she was happy to give me his lawyer's phone number.

Siegi and I then set up a conference call with the attorney. We told him we would like to talk to Josef and something of our plan to help his client. Naturally, this required us talking directly to him at a certain point.

The lawyer knew that the 50 odd pages Joseph had written in jail and his cooperation with the authorities had brought him contempt and animosity from many other people in the industry. It was clear that the devices he had used to hide his tax liabilities and the methodologies he had suggested for control over the industry had clear implications for other vendors' stratagems.

WE WAITED UNEASILY FOR THE ATTORNEY'S CALL, KNOWING THAT NO MATTER WHAT HAPPENED, THE ROAD BEFORE US WOULD NOT BE EASY.

With nobody talking, this opened a Pandora's box for everyone, if not for now, then for the future of an industry already cash-starved by the Tax Agency revenues. Its policy was not grounded on reasonably taxable income based on actual sales or winnings, but on the vendor's investment in each machine, depriving many of the vendors of a true net profit and driving them into the hole with no successful strategies.

Unfortunately, during my career in Austria, the tax system and the social system were completely unreal. The scale had tipped in the opposite direction, strangling the entrepreneur's ability to create the cash needed for investment and growth. This platform of control extended to many industries and truly strangled the motivation of entrepreneurial genius, so necessary for the proper direction of growth of the general economy.

(In my case, mainly because of this unfair tax system—I would eventually elect to move to Monaco and become a permanent resident.)

But my complaint goes even further—into a subtler realm of analysis.

When a government becomes intensely socialist and begins to intrude on the survivability of entrepreneurial innovation and organization, it also can easily develop a particular mindset by the authorities who become agents of this type of government control.

These authorities become a bit like gods to themselves, their legal actions protected by the state, their illegal actions difficult to counter even with costly legal intervention.

This is also true in America, where adequately defending oneself against either a criminal charge or civil complaint, sometimes forces individuals to capitulate against his or her own interest because he or she cannot afford a proper legal remedy.

In this situation, everyone is subject to survival strategies with a built-in temptation to skirt the letter of the law, both on the part of the authorities and of a citizen trying to survive in the case of an unfair economic stranglehold on personal business activities.

This is what happened to the slot industry. And this is why Siegi and I, in deciding to help Josef—and ourselves—were put in the crossfire between the tax authorities and the Austrian slot machine owners.

In reviewing our conversation with the lawyer that night, we drank a lot of Jack and Cokes and, again, realized the high cost and risk of our plan to enter into the "Big Game," using Josef Kammer's assets as leverage.

Over the next few days, we waited uneasily for the attorney's call, knowing that no matter what happened, the road before us would not be easy.

# 33

# Executing the "Plan"

*If anything helped me in my entrepreneurial journey,
it was the ability to take risks for purposes beyond
my own personal interest.*

A couple of days later, we got a call from Josef's lawyer who surprisingly told us we could pick him up from the jail in Vienna on Sunday at 6:00 AM. I thought that was a very peculiar time to release someone from jail.

I had my gun with me, but I was not really concerned. Most of the time I carried it as a general precaution. I felt more secure to be armed.

Siegi and I chose to use fear as our leverage to get Josef to comply with our requests. This would not be difficult because he had already proved his cowardice in dealing with the authorities. And the reality was that he actually had a lot to be afraid of, both from the authorities who had mercilessly used and lied to him, and from the vendors, who frankly hated him.

I got Siegi from his apartment in Baden at 5:00 AM and drove my Mercedes 500 to the First District jail in Vienna for our 6 AM pickup.

We got there on time and waited across the street, staring at the mammoth jail door. Ten minutes later, we recognized him with a big frown on his face, guardedly exiting the jail.

He was the only one who came out of jail on that morning. His betrayal had paid off, at least, for the time being. The reason they let him go was easy. He could say nothing anymore. They knew he was finished. I was really curious which story he would tell us when we finally spoke.

Right then, I flashed back to the time I had left jail after three horrible weeks of intimidation and interrogation. I remember my delight when I saw Tony Zach waiting for me with Herta. But I also remember my bitterness about what had happened and my concern, even paranoia, about what the future held. Yes, I knew exactly how Josef felt right now. Scared and kind of pissed.

But his circumstances were not the same. He didn't have a good friend and his fiancé waiting for him as I had. Rather, two slot vendors who he barely knew who wanted his business.

YOU COULD ALMOST TANGIBLY FEEL HIS FEAR AND NERVOUSNESS.

When he first sidled out the door, Siegi and I immediately crossed the street. This had to have been a freaking funny picture.

Siegi and I had Persian fur coats on, each worth about $15,000. Josef Kammer, the slot machine millionaire fresh out of jail, was not wearing a coat and it was ridiculously cold outside. He had just a suit on, looking just like I remembered him when he came into our office to buy our business—sloppy and scruffy.

We took him between us and walked to my car. I was six feet tall and Siegi, 6'3", while Josef Kammer was maybe 5'3". We must have looked like oversized bouncers or bodyguards for a mafia boss with our gold chains and Persian fur coats. When I think of this picture today, I still have to smile. Whoever saw us would have had to think the same.

For a moment, I felt sorry for him, finally getting out of jail and walking into the arms of strangers who wanted to own his business. You could almost tangibly feel his fear and nervousness.

When we got to the car, I immediately opened the trunk, I retrieved my spare windbreaker that I always kept handy in case the weather turned freezing. Of course, the jacket was too big for him, but at least he was not freezing to death.

Trying to ignore his laughable appearance, we then asked him where he would like to go at this hour of his release.

"I don't know," he said, "but I would like a good coffee and something sweet to chew on. You can't imagine what prison food is like."

I smiled to myself when he said that, then looked at my Rolex. It was just after 6:00 AM and the only place open at this time were hotels.

Then I remembered my last visit to a hotel in Vienna with Karli. It would be a good stylish aftermath to get the taste of prison out of his less-than-pristine mouth.

"I know exactly the right place, Josef. We're going to the Hotel Sacher, the most famous hotel in Vienna with the greatest chocolate torte you'll ever taste."

"Okay," Josef said sheepishly.

"This is the perfect place," I said enthusiastically, "to celebrate our new future together."

He sort of cocked an eyebrow slightly when I said this. And why shouldn't he? Were we really his friends? Probably not. But maybe a marriage of convenience, at least.

Looking at the shivering, chubby little man, I realized what a strange concoction of a character he was.

First of all, he was a man totally dedicated to business, more so in some ways than Siegi or me, because he had nothing else in his life. This, taken alone, was very admirable and was a good reason for his climb to power.

Second, considering the risks he took to get there, including his extremely aggressive attitude toward his competitors, he did have a certain amount of courage as well as stupidity.

But to the world, in a way, courage does involve a kind of stupidity, because taking risks that might cost you your life or security, often does fly in the face of reason.

The best thing I can say about Josef Kammer is that he was an authentic entrepreneur, a risk taker who knew how to make money—admirable in itself. He was really a kind of genius who in only a short time had created an imperious organization. I had no clue how he could fuck himself so badly.

His power came mostly out of excessive, focused greed and his uncanny ability to read the hearts of potential customers and employees providing them with the material things they needed to feel happy, secure and successful. That's how he obtained a great business manager, a loyal group of very intelligent and capable employees, and a very happy set of restaurant and game room owners. Greed fueled his motivation but it wasn't enough to carry him to true independence and self-esteem because, although he knew how to satisfy people's material needs, he did not understand people at all. He was too selfish; and that was his Achilles' heel.

If anything helped me in my entrepreneurial journey, it was the ability to take risks for purposes beyond my own personal interest. Yes, there was egotism there, the egotism of an adventurer or inventor, but not the egotism of a predator like Josef Kammer.

I saw myself as part of the industry, not as a tiger roaming around the Austrian slot machine business, longing to eat every competitor I could find. Siegi and I looked at everyone else as colleagues, I always thought there was room for us and other vendors in the business.

But, in addition to having a different approach to risk-taking than Josef, I also deeply cared about people, not just for what they could do for me, despite what some people said.

Josef Kammer's capitulation to the authorities, without even assessing the protection his employees had provided him by their courageous silence, was proof to me that one of his major character flaws was his absence of the kind of self-esteem that produces real courage. Selfishness enables you on the one hand, but blinds you in another.

And true courage, I believe, comes from another level, one's own personal connection to "Source." And that's the only real security there is.

If Josef had real courage, he would have believed enough in himself and his ability to survive that he could have kept silent himself. But when fear is your ever-present companion, you don't see clearly and ignore the opportunities that are all around you.

Also he would never have delivered the real set of books and betrayed with that action his employees, too. His own secretary

> IT SEEMED LIKE HE WAS FRANTICALLY TRYING TO CHANGE OUR MINDS ABOUT HIM.

was much tougher than him. They examined her for hours and she said nothing. Only when Josef came to the office with them and told her to show them where she hid the books, did she do it.

Also, if he had been able to take note of the reality of his situation, he wouldn't have created a 50 plus page suicide bomb that might take down everyone in the entire industry.

And so I reflected, as we swiftly drove along with little traffic on an early Sunday morning.

Upon arriving at the Ringstrasse, I showed Josef my two Beer Mugs as we passed them by on the way to the hotel.

Now, he started to talk quickly, spouting words out like a machine gun, in a scared, high-pitched voice. Where did he think we were taking him? We were already in the middle of Vienna. We were ten minutes from our destination. Nonetheless, it seemed like he was frantically trying to change our minds about him, chattering almost crazily about how brave he was in jail, how he stood up to his prosecutors, and how he sacrificed himself for the sake of the industry.

It was a sales story that we knew was largely false, except about the reality of his interrogation and its probable harshness. Not only did we know, but everyone in the industry knew, Josef had spilled everything.

Siegi and I said nothing, but we both mouthed "bullshit" to each other when he was looking out the window.

Many of the other vendors—his colleagues in slots—were still in jail. Not one of them had been a canary; not one of them had sung about others' practices. And they could find nothing against them.

As I listened to all this, I was happy that the hotel was not too far away. I knew that, whatever we said, it had to be impressive and powerful at the beginning. And, whatever we wound up doing, it had to be a big enough bite of his business cake to be worth our time.

CHAPTER

# 34

# The Pitch

*If you don't want to listen to us, we will take
you home—safely and unharmed.*

As we moved quickly through the hotel lobby, his gait and demeanor were tell-tale signs of "jail shock," which made him look down somewhat as he shuffled awkwardly to the restaurant. "Jail shock," as I knew so well, destroys your self-confidence and it also destroys your ability to trust people. Although fear might be a component in his motivation to work with us, it was important that he must somehow look at us as a benefit.

Yes, I was willing to stretch a bit to get his mind focused on giving us a chance to partner with him. But I also know that whatever picture I painted for him about the dangerous course he had taken in releasing the secrets of the industry to the authorities, it was the blatant truth!

Did my approach with him cross some kind of line?

Well, maybe. I did watch too many American gangster films when I was younger and maybe I could have chosen a slightly different approach.

> "HEY, I DID A LOT FOR THIS INDUSTRY."

But my own house of cards was getting caught in a tsunami, and I acted out of bravado and desperation for saving our own business, an event that did not totally temper my actions with the greatest possible cordiality. In other words, I decided to strong arm the little son-of-a-bitch.

Would I do the same today? For sure not. But this is what I did back then.

I parked in front of the Hotel Sacher and gave the key to the valet.

We chose a table where we thought we could talk quietly without distraction. We all ordered breakfast and Josef also added a Sacher torte, a Coke and a coffee.

If I were in a better mood, I might have found Josef's table manners more amusing. But, at the time, Siegi and my eyes only widened in horror as the poor little fellow bolted down his food like a famished wild pig. When he was finished with this display of gastronomical ardor, a spectacle of unashamed open mouth chewing punctuated by tiny, regular explosions of saliva across the table, Siegi and I barely had the stomach to start our breakfast.

Once he began chomping on the torte and slurping up his coffee, we began our sales pitch.

"Look, Josef, you probably know that the very best thing that can happen is that by using us as partners, you will leave the industry with only a black eye. Because if you stay in, like you probably intend to do ..."

"So you say. Hey, I did a lot for this industry. I protected those owners. I stood up for everybody."

"Stood up for them?" Siegi said. "By spilling your goddamn guts out?"

"I didn't put the finger on nobody."

"No, you just wrote a 50-page paper that could break every goddamn person in the vending industry. And on top of it, you told them you had a second bookkeeping set and with that you fucked not only yourself, but you also fucked all your customers and your employees, too."

I put my arm on Siegi's and said quietly, "He just got out of jail. Give him a break!"

I then noticed a small but remarkable thing—a tear or two glistening in Josef's eyes. Maybe we were instinctively playing good cop-bad cop. And Josef was actually moved by my small act to quiet Siegi down. It was probably the only kindness he had experienced from anyone in weeks.

Siegi was pretty hot under the collar and started to get up. I shook my head, first slightly, then vigorously. He sat back down with a sigh.

ONCE IT WAS KNOWN THAT HE WAS OUT, ALL KINDS OF THINGS COULD HAPPEN.

"Siegi wants you to see it the way the vendors and your customers see it. He wants you to wake up to reality. To give the tax authorities your books, they have it now in black and white, all the names and all the numbers."

"If you'd been where I've been, you might have a different idea altogether about reality, Sitter," Josef said.

"I have been," I said, looking directly in his eyes. "And I don't mean for a couple of days."

At that point, I seemed to catch his attention. But time was running out. Once it was known that he was out, all kinds of things could happen and everyone, including the government, might have ideas on how to use him. We had to make an impression fast.

Still hoping to eat my breakfast, I took a mouthful or two, but then gave up and started to talk to Josef again saying, "Look, Josef, you must know by now that you fucked up badly!"

"I heard your accusations and your interpretation, but think about it. They are going to put things in order in the system and they asked me to help them. Considering everything, why should I refuse?"

"You're kidding me, right!" I said.

"No, I'm not. My lawyer said that everything's fixable, nobody's really hurt, and my cooperation will help everyone."

"Listen to me, Josef, I'm not bullshitting you. I'm not some damn revenue officer or a lawyer wanting to yank your money away from you and shove it in his pocket."

"What makes you so different from them?"

"My motives are pure," I said.

Josef started to laugh. Even Siegi was startled by it. It started as a low chortle, but then preceded to uncontrollable laughter, like he was reacting to a good joke. But then it morphed to an almost hysterical whine of laughter, forcing me to I looked around to see if we were attracting too much attention. But there was only an older couple in the corner of the room, holding hands, totally oblivious of us. For a moment, I was transfixed and touched by the two of them.

When he ceased laughing, he glared at me, "You two really want to steal my company, don't you?"

"No, Josef, we're trying to help you."

"Talk about bullshit …"

"You don't get it, Josef …"

"Yes, you'd like to own my company, discredit me in front of the authorities and the vending companies—first—before you fucking gun me down. I see the rod you're carrying, Sitter. I'd have to be a damn fool to miss it. You're here to scare me and then take away my business."

"I carry large amounts of money with me every day. I need the gun."

"Bullshit. We're in a hotel in the middle of the city."

"Okay, Josef, we're probably not the only people who know you're out of prison. And the fact is, if certain people even thought we were trying to help you, they might try to off all of us. We took a large risk in even taking you here, but at least it's a public place."

"GET YOUR ASS BACK HERE. WE'RE NOT FINISHED!"

Josef smirked and then said, "Sure," and pointed to the older couple adding, "yeah, real public."

"To tell you the truth, we don't have much time. So, if you don't want to listen to us, we will take you home—safely and unharmed. And, if we see you again, we will wave and say hello, but there will be no chance we will consider doing business with you."

"Sure," he said with that same skeptical look on his face.

"We're leaving, Siegi," and I slowly got up, flipping some paper and coins onto the table for the waiter.

Josef just sat there, confused and then said, "Sit down, Sitter. I didn't come here for chitchat. I came here because my lawyer told me to. What is your damn proposal?"

"I'm leaving, Josef." And Siegi started to amble over to the door while I searched for more change.

Josef furrowed his brow and yelled across the room to Siegi, so loud that even the elderly couple looked up. "Get your ass back here. We're not finished!"

Siegi shrugged and slowly ambled back, and I pushed the money over to the side of the table. Once we were again seated, I leaned over the table and looked directly at Josef.

"Siegi and I will try to save your ass, but if you think everyone should canonize you or award you with some kind of a goddamn medal, then we should do you a favor and take you over to nearest psycho ward."

"I tried to do ...," Josef muttered.

Siegi shot a stern look directed at Josef and said, "Shut up and listen to Hans. We want to be out of here as soon as we can."

"Well, maybe I shouldn't have written that paper ..."

"You're right, but maybe your lawyer could fix that part. He could say you were forced to do so. He also could say they beat the hell out of you, so you did everything they asked to make them stop. But to give them your books, there is no way out for you anymore. You are really fucked now. You were free, stupid. None of your employees said a goddamn thing, but now you have given them all the ammunition they need to screw everyone into the fucking wall."

"Well, I didn't mean to ..."

"So, are you getting what Hans is saying?" Siegi said. "Everybody in the fucking industry hates you."

"Maybe ...," he said.

"Maybe ...?" Siegi said, looking at the ceiling, evincing total contempt for his stupidity.

"This is no time for denial, Josef. You need to believe us when I tell you that everyone—I mean everyone—in the industry hates you," I said, reiterating Siegi's statement of truth.

"Well, I guess ..."

"Guess nothing. Do you believe it?" I said staring him down.

"Yes," he said in a meek voice. "It's probably true."

"Good," I said. "Then get this: Siegi and I are offering you a one-way ticket to come out of all of this in one piece, but not if you aren't honest with yourself. Because not only does the industry hate you, so do the prosecutors and the agency AND SPECIFICALLY YOUR CUSTOMERS."

"Did they tell you that they would let you go immediately if you helped them?"

"Yes, but ..."

"But nothing. They lied to your face."

"They needed ..."

"They needed nothing, Josef," Siegi said. "They needed to make sure you told them everything before they let you go."

"Did you have a fun time when they held you?"

"No, they sat on my head every day. They kept the lights on; they kept me from sleeping."

"In other words, they treated you like a goddamn criminal, not their trusted ally?"

"Yes."

Siegi looked at him. "So wake up, stupid. Listen to Hans. You don't go to a doctor and then tell him you don't have any pain. How can he help you if you do that?"

"All right, I don't trust them. They are bastards."

"So, when you go to a doctor, you tell him where the pain is coming from so he can help you. Right now, I'm ... we're your doctors." And Siegi smiled for the first time.

"They might put me back in jail. They left the door open. There was a certain ambiguity."

"That's right. They're not done with you, unless you can somehow get the jump on them."

"Okay, I see that," Josef responded.

"Right now, because of your stupid paper, and your books, everyone is expecting an audit, and that audit could be very inconvenient for a lot of us. It's not even a question of if ... it's a question of when."

Josef sighed.

"A lot of people would like to shut you up permanently. Siegi and I have a strategy, a way to protect you ..."

"Shit."

# 35

# Agreement

*I was watching him like a hawk, our prey tangled in
sagebrush and cactus, the complex web of fear and guilt
that immobilized his reasoning and made him
doubly vulnerable to suggestion.*

"This goes both ways, Josef. Because if we go out of the way
for you, we don't expect to be fucked."

His eyes widened. "No, if we agree, I will not do anything to
you. I think you know my reputation."

"Yes, it's true, you little prick," Siegi said. "You do keep your
promises."

Josef stared at him, obviously not liking the derogatory
comment.

"We can be civil, Siegi. Apologize to him. That was not
necessary."

Siegi mumbled, "Okay, maybe you're not a little prick—
maybe a big prick," he smiled.

I looked at Josef, who looked skyward and smiled ... just a little.

Suddenly, the restaurant door flung open and a group of people came in and sat down. They were quickly followed by a man in a long leather overcoat who sat down at a different table, picked up the menu, then looked around the room. He had a grim expression on his face.

Josef looked at him and in seconds, his mood changed. With his eyes wide-open and lower lip hanging down, he turned his head toward me. I saw panic and fear spread across his face.

At first, I didn't get it. Then I realized, he thinks that the guy wearing the leather coat might be an assassin. *Shit,* I said to myself. *Maybe I scared him too much! I don't want him to leave.*

"He's probably just a goddamn stockbroker, whose cranky because he hasn't had breakfast."

Then, in a stroke of genius, Siegi did a very smart thing. He got up, grabbed a paper from one of the tables, and sat right next to Leather Overcoat.

Feeling he was now protected, Josef turned to me and said, "All right, let's get to it!"

Now I had him, finally, after all this shit. Like a good poker player or a wolf that had his prey cornered, now was the time to pounce. But it had to be the right kind of pounce, not one that scared him too much or too little. If I did it right, Siegi and I could make an almost instantaneous fortune.

Picture a brain, once dull and gray, now glowing with excitement, oozing sparks of light, pulsating rhythmically, even orgasmically, with anticipation. That was my brain at the moment, working to process everything I knew and understood about Josef at the speed of light.

"Lawyers aren't so friendly when they're not getting paid."

He is small and slimy, I thought, but not stupid. He is a victim of what has been traditionally called "the little man syndrome," where a little man, like Emperor Napoleon, Actor Humphrey Bogart or the French President, Nicolas Sarkozy, was said to be compensating for his stature by adding a certain extra amount of aggression to his actions and character.

Another point was that owing to his slovenliness and lack of self-esteem, he really had no friends, and no girlfriend. All he had were his employees, his business and his cash flow. It is in this sad deficit to his life, I saw our opportunity.

I took a breath and said, "Don't fool yourself, Josef. If you don't partner up with somebody, you will lose everything."

"I don't see that. Why?" he said.

"You really don't get it, do you?"

"I suppose not, but I'm listening."

"First of all, this so-called Tax Agency is not your friend. The tax agents have proved it by lying to you about freeing you and then keeping you in prison. They have the power, now that you have confessed, to take all of your money and your vending and slot machines."

"Then I will fight them," he said quietly.

"Lawyers aren't so friendly when they're not getting paid."

"True," Josef acknowledged, nodding his head slightly.

"So, whether or not you use a high-priced lawyer, you will get your crack at justice, maybe only a few years from now. There is an ongoing investigation and prosecutors can always use that as an excuse. By delaying, it hurts your cash flow and makes you more defenseless and unable to sustain your little battle with them to get back your assets," I continued. "Even before they do seize anything, things may have to settle down a bit. They also need you now for any prosecutions that may go down. They may temporarily treat you as a 'friendly witness,' but that probably will not last. To them, you are expedient. Actually, this delay can work mightily to your advantage because with it, we will have enough time to act."

"But what if they don't take my assets? What if I were able to keep it all? What if you are wrong?"

"My plan will help you no matter what you do. You assume that the tax revenue office is your only problem ..."

"... I'd say they're a pretty big problem," Josef cut in.

"And I'd say you're correct there, but, truthfully, the bigger problem is the state of mind of your competitors. Believe me— they hate you. They are after you, my friend, and unless you do something, they will figure out a way to hunt you down and nail you to a wall."

"And that something that you want me to do, I'm betting it has something to do with you and your partner?"

"GOOD GOD, JOSEF, DO YOU HAVE A BRAIN?"

"Yes. Someone to take the heat away from you and negotiate with your competitors from a position that is beneficial to your interests."

"I don't know."

"Well, let me explain then. When you wrote your 50 pages, you probably didn't realize that the content was released almost immediately after you put your name on it. We know that they told you that if you helped them, you would become the Casino Czar of Austria, in charge of monitoring all your competitors' cash flow. You would soon become 'Josef Kammer, a government institution.'"

"What's so bad about that?"

"Good God, Josef, do you have a brain? These are your competitors, whose secrets you summed up on those 50 pages. You exposed and endangered everyone with the inconvenience of an audit, the ruination of their business and the possibility of jail. And worse, you make yourself personally responsible for monitoring these guys and possibly turning them in! Don't you get it?"

Finally, Josef seemed to grasp what I was saying. There was an "Oh, shit!" expression spreading across his face.

"Oh, yes ... and don't forget, you also told the revenue officers how you gave Greg, your general manager, two million dollars to buy him out and then advised him to send his money out of the country—to a Swiss bank! So, in ratting on him, you screwed your closest employee by betraying him. What the hell were you thinking? Can you imagine what that guy would like to do to you?

"Besides all the things they asked you, you volunteered a lot of shit, stories about people you never needed to reveal. Prisoners in jail call people like you RATS."

As we talked, I could see Siegi getting angrier and angrier. I guess my words were igniting some of the deeply hostile feelings he felt for Josef. I was being strategic but Siegi was turning red.

"I guess you told them when you take a dump in the morning and which toothpaste you use," he blurted out.

Upon Siegi's outburst, Josef began to fall apart. His face started to get redder, his lower lip dropped a bit more, and he started to pant uncontrollably. I had never really seen a person so suddenly and so completely gripped by fear in such a short period of time.

He said, "How do you know? I couldn't help it. They wanted everything—EVERYTHING! They never let up! They never let me alone!"

## The Deal Is Put in Motion

I was watching him like a hawk, our prey tangled in sagebrush and cactus, the complex web of fear and guilt that immobilized his reasoning and made him doubly vulnerable to suggestion.

Was this right ... the set up I created with Siegi to take down Josef's business? Would I look at things this way now? No, but back then, I did not want to give him one second of space to recover his faculties. It was time to pounce!

"Yes, you did wrong. Yes, people may be after you. But in my opinion, and in Siegi's, everything you actually did can be righted. We have a plan, Josef! And if you do exactly what we tell you, we'll save your ass. But if you try to fuck us like the others, then you have a real problem. Trust me on that one. We are not going to save your ass, be handed a "thank you note" by you, and then be betrayed by you. That would be your biggest mistake. Then, you are really finished. I promise you."

Josef cleared his throat and asked in a muted voice, "What should I do?"

"We will need to create a new corporation. Your current company, 'Josef Kammer's Vending,' will sell everything to the new corporation, with payment coming from us to be made monthly.

"For the next two years, because of the sale, you will derive a monthly income of $40,000. That's correct and we will see when it's more, we split the money 50/50—don't worry. Your explanation will be: 'I've had enough—I'm scared and don't want to be in this business anymore.'

"Here's what will happen: you will have a trustee in Switzerland or Liechtenstein who holds your 50 percent part in the new company. The way we will establish this will be completely legal and that's it."

At this point, his eyes widened again, but he didn't say anything.

> "DON'T WORRY, JOSEF, WE *WILL* WATCH OUT FOR YOU."

"In the meantime, I will give you the phone number of a well-respected CPA, famous in the most reputable business circles in Austria, who is well connected to the Tax Agency. He will help your lawyer work out a deal with the tax officials."

"Go over it again for me, please."

"Okay, you get $40,000 a month for the sale of your original company and, on the other hand, you will be our silent partner in the new company.

"We will transfer money to you every month along with the numbers from the counter mechanisms, so you will know the exact income from the money. You know how that works; you gave all the paperwork to the tax officers. Every month we will send it to your trustee. The deal itself will be completely legal. While this is going on, Siegi and I will take the heat both from the Tax Agency and their audits and the fights with your competitors. This is a great deal for you, a totally win-win situation. We can all start making money tomorrow even while you act like a submarine, diving well below everyone's field of vision, while Siegi and I fight off the first wave of attacks by the agency and your angry vendors. At some point, when the heat is gone, maybe you can choose to re-emerge."

Josef was nervous, sliding around on his chair with sweat trickling down his forehead. He looked in my eyes, cleared his throat and said with a husky voice, "Okay, I will do it. You know what I've been through, and I get what you think of me. I hope you are honorable and will not hold anything against me as an excuse to screw me over."

As conversation went back and forth between Josef and me, Siegi didn't say anything. He watched us closely and quietly, not adding anything to it. He hated Josef deeply, and I suspected, would in the future. My gut told me that whatever relationship evolved would be on me.

At that moment, I felt kind of sorry for him. Look what we were doing. We were about to take his company away from him with no cash up front and make a mega deal for ourselves. We viewed the risk for ourselves as nominal.

This was the first time in my life I ever appreciated our powerful Austrian Tax Agency. They had destroyed Josef Kammer, but put Siegi and me in the Big Game.

Josef tried now to make eye contact with Siegi. And Siegi, to my surprise, despite the disdainful look on his face, did manage to reach out to shake Josef's sweaty hand.

Whatever the case, Siegi's next words were surprisingly diplomatic. "I'm glad for your sake that you were smart enough to make that deal with us. It will help you recover quickly from the shock of all this crap."

He then said something with a kind of authentic ring. Maybe he had, in fact, garnered a little bit of sympathy for Josef or at least began to recognize what our agreement might mean to both of us.

"Don't worry, Josef, we will watch out for you."

I looked at Siegi in surprise, and then shook Josef's hand as well. "Really, don't worry," amplifying Siegi's promise, "everything will be okay!"

We then paid the tab and left the Sacher Café.

CHAPTER

# 36

# Take Over Plans

*I braced in anticipation, hoping that the golden palace was indeed the destination, but ready for any changes and surprises along the way.*

On the way home, we made our plans to begin the first stages of organizing Josef's businesses. We decided to meet at his office the next day at 11:00 AM and take a look.

We had to learn the best route to take, to effectively manage all of his locations, interact with his employees and introduce ourselves as the new owners of the company. We would let them know that Josef was only going to be around for a few weeks to help make the transfer as easy as possible.

Of course, the biggest problem we had would be with all the game room and restaurant owners, where he had placed his slot machines. Every single one of these unfortunate citizens, owing to Josef's deft mouth in jail and his double bookkeeping records, was probably expecting a particularly unpleasant audit.

Then when he originally split the money with the owners, it was clear that Josef told them how to disguise their true income. This was the core of his confession to the authorities, and, undoubtedly, it was how he let loose a deadly volley of tax grenades directed at everyone involved with him in business. Siegi and I realized that this level of money had challenges—managing slot machines at multiple locations was never all that easy and we had to step up to the plate right away.

> "IT COULD BE A MEGA DEAL, BUT WE HAVE TO ACT VERY CAREFULLY."

To get everything under control, I had to alert my employees at the car business and to Mr. Pelts, who ran the restaurant/game rooms, that I would be tied up for a few weeks while I got everything under control. At this point, I thought I might need an assistant manager to support his efforts. To organize Josef's company was definitely going to require a huge effort.

En route to taking Josef to his office, where his parents had a house and a restaurant and where he headquartered, I pointed out my car lot in Vienna. He already knew I had a number of different businesses and maybe that was one of the main reasons he thought partnering with us had some credibility.

When we hit the Autobahn, I sped up, pushing my AMG Mercedes 500 as fast as possible. His home town was forty miles south of Vienna. With no traffic and at 150 mph, we made it in short order.

Believe it or not, we began to find some common ground between the three of us. In fact, we had one thing in common: we each had grown up in the restaurant business with each of our parents owning their own restaurant. That was a remarkable coincidence, I thought.

After we dropped him off at his home, I took Siegi back to his apartment. Finally, we could talk privately.

"What do you think, Siegi?" I asked.

He said, "I think it could be a mega deal, but we have to act very carefully. First of all, we will be on the Tax Agency's radar with this question: 'What the fuck do we have to do with Josef?' On the other hand, we have to deal with all of his competitors. They really hate his guts; because of that, they now may hate our guts.

"Also, we have to go to each of his restaurant and game room owners and convince them we are not the same assholes. That will be a tough call, Hans. That idiot fucked everybody. The Agency had no proof of any wrongdoing. I can understand why they would want to beat the shit out of him. But my brother and I will take care of it."

I was very happy about his willingness to step up to the plate, a plate that could be extremely violent and dangerous, but I also had my responsibilities in this takeover.

"Look, Siegi, this was my idea. It's my fight too. I'm not going to let you and your brother take all the heat. I'll be there if we get in trouble.

"Frankly, I don't think anything will start now because everyone in the business has to watch his back, especially from the Tax Agency. That works in our favor. The sad story is all the others are still in jail, and I'm really sorry for them. But for us, right now it is an absolute advantage. If they were not in jail right now, they would go to every place of Kammer's and we would lose a lot of places, believe me.

"Think about how it all went down, Siegi. It was not more than a year ago that Josef came with his partner, Greg, to buy our business and we refused. And now, without any real cash outlay, we are partners in this mammoth business. All we had to really put on the table was our fearlessness."

"Shit, it's hard to believe," Siegi said, "how fast everything can change."

I'm also amazed. "This is a different world for us now. If we act carefully, without making any mistakes, taking care to provoke no one, I believe we can keep the tax officers and the vendors happy and keep the competitors at bay."

"At least everyone will be happy to get rid of him," Siegi said.

"That's true," I said. "But, you know, our silent partner has some assets, which I think we should appreciate. Now having talked to him and seen his organization for a few weeks, I think it's fair to say he is unbelievably smart. He knows everything about slot machines—right there, a great asset. And, he has developed a really good organization by keeping his promises to his employees and paying them well."

"Too bad he is a fucking coward and a rat," Siegi said.

"I don't want to give him any credit, but do we really know what happened to him in prison? Every situation is different. I would say he is a coward and a rat, too, but I would also say that he feels bad about what he did. He obviously didn't think it through."

"Sounds like you're trying to find excuses for him."

"No, Siegi, not excuses. Just trying not to hate the one person in my life who may perhaps enrich you—and me—separately and collectively beyond anyone else in our lives. I'm just hoping the little bit of credit I'm giving him will not turn to dust in a heartbeat if he doesn't keep his promises to us."

"That's the ticket, my friend. Give him all the goddamn credit you want, but watch our backs."

> **WOW, WHAT DAY IS IT?**

"I never said I have given him my trust. I know he could turn on us."

"If he does, that's the last mistake he'll ever make," Siegi said.

I turned onto the street where Siegi lived. Before he got out, he smiled and said, "Come on, have a drink and we can play billiards. Best of three for a hundred bucks."

"Why not? Gives me a chance to beat your ass."

We both laughed and went inside. We played billiards mixed with a bit of conversation and, as usual when playing Siegi, I lost my hundred bucks.

It was now 11:30 AM. I called Herta and told her I would be home in time to have lunch together. On the way home, I thought, *Lunch will be on time, but—wow, what day is it?*

---

What a crazy life I had. Crazy, yes, but boring, never! I saw myself again on the roller coaster called Life. For a moment, the roller coaster had stopped and I had taken a break, playing billiards with a friend, getting ready to have lunch with my wife. In effect, I was throwing a few balls at a clown and munching on some cotton candy, while the carnival engineers checked each car of the coaster to see if it was safe.

Soon, very soon, I knew I would take my place in the front seat of the coaster again, and be hurtled forward, up and down—at an immense speed!

Where was I going? Nowhere in particular; it really didn't matter. The ride itself was the goal.

Right then, I felt the roller coaster calling me. The shape of the cars had changed and the sculptured face on the lead car had changed from a winsome siren to someone who looked very much like Josef Kammer. Not very appealing, I thought, but if I was right, this roller coaster was heading me toward a very large golden palace.

I braced in anticipation, hoping that the golden palace was indeed the destination, but ready for any changes and surprises along the way.

It was very early Monday morning when I literally jumped out of bed and headed to the office at lightning speed. In general, I liked to be there ahead of everybody else, so I could plan for the day. But this time, I had to plan for the next few weeks, a critical time for helping to redesign and rebuild Josef's organization. I was hungry now for clarity, direction and the ability to act immediately on my conclusions.

Besides solving the problem with Josef, I had to streamline my own company's management. All this had to be accomplished quickly and thoroughly.

Once I had a planning session alone in my office, I would have a critical management meeting for my own companies. To make sure this happened, I had called my secretary, Christa, at home.

Christa had been with me since I built the office in Theresienfeld. She was the only one who could sign on my business account and was very loyal and trustworthy.

She had scheduled a meeting at 8:00 AM with Vick, Mr. Pelts and all my sales managers from the car business. Of course, I'd asked Christa to take notes at the meeting.

I arrived at my office by 7:00 AM ready for action. I began my morning by making myself a coffee, feeding Harry and Caesar and then retreating upstairs to my private office.

I loved my office, in a way, it was my sanctuary. It was very cozy with mahogany wooden walls, a French-styled white chaise lounge sofa with the gold leaf set in one corner, a fully stocked marble bar with four bar stools in another corner, and a hand-carved wooden conference table with six black leather chairs. There were several fine matching Tabriz Persian area rugs on the floor. The office was filled with photos and bric-a-brac from my travels and entrepreneurial adventures. Christa made sure there were fresh flowers strategically placed for every important meeting.

In addition to my office upstairs, I also had a private guest room complete with a bed, a shower and a bathroom where I would stay at times when I thought it was too late to drive home. In the evening, after I had fed them, my dogs would come visit me in my office or the guest room, either lying behind my desk or near the bed, watching over me as I slept. I loved the atmosphere at my office building. It nourished me and gave me a feeling of privacy and peace.

On this particular day, I felt an unusual urgency. I had only an hour to prepare for the meeting and one hour to give my instructions to my staff. After that, I had to pick up Siegi and travel to the "Cave of the Wounded Lion," in other words, to see Josef Kammer.

When my employees arrived for the meeting, I informed them about what was going on. I told them that Siegi and I were going to take over managing Josef Kammer's company.

Kammer's name was quite familiar to everyone there, even if they were not connected at all to our slot business. It was all over the newspapers. Josef Kammer had become quite famous.

I explained that despite his reputation, taking over his business was a gigantic opportunity for all of us, and I needed one hundred percent of their support. I particularly needed it because I was going to have to leave the management of the business to them, and they would have to help each other out, no matter what their particular role usually was.

> "THERE'S A LETTER INSTRUCTING THEM TO CATEGORICALLY HAVE YOU TAKE OVER MY OPERATIONS—IF ANYTHING EVER HAPPENS TO ME."

The meeting ended in high spirits, with everybody assuring me that I could count on them.

As everyone was leaving, I asked Vick if I could speak with him alone before he left. He sat near my desk, patiently waiting until the others had left my interior office.

Then, I turned to him and said, "Listen, Vick, you know I don't just think of you as an employee. More than anything, I regard you as my friend."

"Likewise," he said.

"Vick, I guess it's time to tell you ..."

"Tell me what?" he asked.

"It's a general point, something I decided before Josef became an issue in my life. Something I told my lawyers a long time ago ..."

Vick obviously wasn't sure what to think, so he sat there quietly.

"There's a letter instructing them to categorically have you take over my operations—if anything ever happens to me."

"What the hell? Why are you telling me now?"

"Because I don't know exactly what will happen."

"Do you think you will go to jail with this bullshit, then don't do it."

"I don't know. But it is an opportunity to beat the hell out of me and Siegi. There are some really angry people out there who could lose everything because of Kammer's big mouth. They might want us out, too."

A long silence stretched between us.

"Shut up, Hans."

"Try and look at this in a positive way. Maybe it's only my way to tell you how much I appreciate what you've done for me, your loyalty and dedication. And how much I really love you."

Vick, who I know cared for me as well, now said nothing. It was as if he were shell-shocked.

I gave him a hug and he said, "Don't worry, I will take care of everything around here. But please take care of yourself. Take nothing for granted."

"I'll be careful," I said.

I felt very good after that conversation.

CHAPTER

# 37

# Betrayal

*I braced in anticipation, hoping that the golden palace was indeed the destination, but ready for any changes and surprises along the way.*

I was so happy; everything looked great. It is unbelievable what we created with that deal with Josef and I already saw how much money we would make.

It was like a lotto win for Siegi and me. I guessed we could make at least a million dollars every month, a big change from just surviving right now, to making a real profit and with plenty of cash flow. I felt like I was the King of the World. I touched my gun, took it out from my holster and looked at it.

It was funny looking at the enchased gold letters of my name and my birthday. This was a present from my third week of marriage. One of Anton's hobbies was collecting weapons; one day he said, "Could you give me your gun for a couple of days. I know your birthday is coming up and I have a surprise for you. You can have my Glock in exchange; I know you feel naked without your gun."

He gave me his Glock and holster and he took my pistol and on my birthday he returned my gun and said, "I sent your gun to a weapon specialist and he enchased the contours by the clip with your name and birth date in 24 carat gold."

I really loved my gun; it was a special weapon—unique and nothing like it.

I looked at "her," stroked her, pressed the pistol to my lips and said, "I guess you saved me already a couple of times, friend." I don't know why, but right now I wanted to take a closer look at my 38 special. I put her back in my holster and my thoughts returned to our mega deal with Josef.

I made myself an espresso and thought again how close I was to losing everything, and now—yes, yes—everything has worked out perfectly. We would have 1,600 more slot machines; a company with an estimated value of at least nine million dollars would be under our control; and half of that company would be ours—Siegi's and mine. What a deal. I went downstairs whistling a song, feeling so fucking happy and full of energy. Thinking about our deal ... amazing. I started to yell, yes, yes, YES! I raised a fist high in the air and screamed, "We did it. Johann Sitter, you are invincible, you are the greatest...! We did it...!"

I then left my office and headed out to pick up Siegi at the Airplane Bar. Soon we were on our way to see Josef, arriving at his office exactly on time. With a sense of pleasant anticipation, we entered his office and said, "Good morning, guys, is Josef here?"

One of the girls said, "No, but you both should talk to his secretary. Ingrid is in the next room."

I thought that was strange, but Siegi and I went in the next room and greeted her. "Hi, Ingrid. Nice to see you again. How are you doing?"

"I'm doing okay."

"Where is Josef? I'm sure he told you we will be taking over his company; we will be working together."

She said, "I'm sorry, Mr. Sitter, but I'm not so sure that plan works out with Josef. He told me, just this morning, he doesn't know what to do. He is on his way to the airport; he is going to his relatives in Canada. He told me also he will get in touch with you as soon as he is there. His plane leaves at 3 PM.

This piece of shit fucked us; that was all I could think right then. I looked at her as though she was an alien. Inside, I felt I was close to having a heart attack. Numbness flowed through my body.

I looked at Siegi and Siegi looked at me—we were speechless.

Standing in front of Ingrid's desk like two big dummies, thousands of thoughts went through my head but the main one was: *I will kill that motherfucker. He screwed us. He gave us his word.*

But it became clearer with her next sentence. She said, "Josef, before he left, said something like the slot machine business is over and the government will take over all the slot machines. That is the reason he didn't want to make the deal with you guys after all. It doesn't matter anymore."

I said, "Which asshole told him that bullshit? That cannot be true at all."

"I don't know, Mr. Sitter. He told us we should continue to operate, and he will give us other instructions in a couple of days."

*I WILL KILL THAT MOTHERFUCKER.*
*HE SCREWED US.*
*HE GAVE US HIS WORD.*

Siegi said, "Come on, let's go, before I destroy this whole fucking office."

Siegi and I turned away, and returned to my car. My head was pounding and I was mad, I mean really don't get in my way mad.

We were so close to saving Josef's ass and making millions together, and now, in a moment, the opposite. I thought, don't panic, be cool. But fuck, I couldn't. Not only did we lose the deal with Josef, but if he was right, and gambling was over, I would really lose everything!

All the business that I had with Siegi provided the main income from our slot machines. Not only that, I used that income to cover my losses from the restaurants and the car business. If Josef was right, then I was in deep shit. And the more I thought about it, the more furious I became.

I started to speed up, forgetting that I was driving through a small town. At the first sharp turn, my car skidded and Siegi said, "Fuck, Hans, you want to kill us?"

I said, "Hell, no, I want to kill that motherfucker. Let him tell me where the hell he got his information. He better have a good answer, or I will cut his throat, or greet him with a bullet between the eyes. That bastard shook our hands and swore he would not break his word, and that's a real contract!"

Flooring the throttle and gunning the engine to the limit, Siegi said, "What the hell, Hans, are you out of your mind? Slow down, or we will not only be broke, we will be dead!"

"I'm sorry, Siegi. I'll take you to your car and then I'll drive to the airport, find that asshole, and cut him to pieces unless he has an answer for me. I will get his ass, if that is the last thing that I do in this world. Nobody leaves me in the rain over a screwed up story. I want to know where he got his info, or he will be history."

My tires squealed as I pressed the throttle down and drove away.

"Don't be stupid, Hans. Calm down. Tomorrow is another day and we will figure something out."

I heard Siegi talking, but I wasn't listening.

I drove crazy fast to the Airplane Bar, let Siegi out and said, "I'm sorry Siegi, I have to find that asshole, or I will explode. My dreams are hollow right now. I am too close to fulfilling my dreams to give up so easily. But that road I have to walk alone. Please don't stop me. I will be careful, but I have to do it. At least I have to try."

"Okay, I hope you know what the hell you are doing. But I'm telling you, don't fuck up your whole life for an asshole," Siegi said and slammed the door. My tires squealed as I pressed the throttle down and drove away.

Gunning the engine again, I drove insanely in the direction of Vienna hitting 150 mph on the Autobahn, and then took an exit that was a shortcut to Schwechat, where the airport for Vienna was located. I drove the narrow road like a wild man, and was ten minutes away from the airport when I passed another 500 Mercedes. Passing it, I could not believe my eyes; it was Josef. I thought: *Oh my god, you are mine now.*

I slowed and set my blinker. I went in front of his car to slow him down and get his attention.

After a few seconds, he saw that I wanted him to stop. He pulled over; I did the same. I felt like I was outside my own head and body, certainly not myself!

He gave me an icy stare. Then a weird feeling came over me that I'd never experienced. I was not myself. I acted like a robot— as if someone else was in control.

Getting out of my car, I walked toward his Mercedes—he opened his door and got out, asking, "What you are doing here?"

I yelled at him saying, "You ask me what I'm doing here. I'll tell you what I'm doing here!"

Without thinking, I walked straight at him as I pulled my gun from its holster. And then remembered the funny feeling I had had that morning as I looked at my gun and saw how magnificent it was. Then I thought: That is more than strange. It was like I was talking to my gun, whispering, I guess I have a job for you.

Josef's eyes got big. He looked at me like I was a ghost. I grabbed him by his hair and pulled him down hard. He screamed like a pig and fell on his knees. I pointed the pistol at his forehead and yelled, "You piece of shit, we had a deal. We had a fucking deal ... Do you know what a deal is ...? Do you know what that means ...? We had a deal ... Now start to pray you will have more than a good excuse and a good source of why you are running away and breaking your word. Who told you that stupid lie that the slot machines are forbidden? Who ...? Who ...?"

I cocked the hammer of my 38 special and at that moment I felt like I was an ice cold monster.

As Josef heard the distinct sound of a cocking pistol, he started crying, and then wailed, "Please, please don't kill me. Please ... I did not want to break my contract with you ... Please ...!

I could barely understand him, as he wept. I demanded, "Who the fuck gave you your information? Talk ... or you will never talk again ... talk asshole.... TALK, TALK ....

"My lawyer, my lawyer said it," and then he cried out, "What should I do? What can I do ...?" ... more weeping and blubbering. "What would you do? I have relatives in Canada, and it's my last chance to start over, to rebuild and take my machines with me. Please, please, let me go.... Please ... don't shoot me ... pleeeeaase ...!"

I heard a car coming. It was as though I was waking from a bad dream. I finally saw the scene: Josef in front of me in the middle of the road, a gun pointed at his head and a car coming that would see us. I could be put away behind bars for 20 years. I was insane; I was really close to hurting that asshole.

> "Drive and don't look back."

I pulled him in front of me, close to my face so I could stare him in his eyes and took the gun from his head. Moments later the car passed slowly by and the driver looked strangely at us. Putting one hand over Josef's shoulder, like we were the best of friends, I looked at the driver and tried to put a smile on my face. As the car drove on, I whispered in his ear, "Run. Run as fast as you can to your car, jump in and drive.

"Drive and don't look back. Run, motherfucker, run. Run for your screwed up life ...."

Josef could only stagger back to his car, still weeping. I stood and looked on in utter disbelief.

CHAPTER

# 38

# End of the Dream

*I don't know how long I lay there, as my brain
slowly began to work again.*

As Josef slowly started to drive away, I shot three times in the
air and saw him speed away when he heard the shots. I stared
after him until I could no longer see him.

I was parked on an embankment that sloped down about 30
feet to a little river and a sandbank. I staggered down in the
direction of the sand bank, gun still in my hand. When I arrived
I fell on my knees and shot the last three bullets into the water.

With every detonation my entire body shook as though hit
by the bullets. When the last bullet was gone, I fell on my back
in the sand, looked up and said, "Oh my God, what the hell is
wrong with me. I was so close to hurting or worse killing that guy.
Oh my God! It was like I woke up from a bad dream. Tears were
running down my face and I stared up at the sky. I saw the clouds
moving by and became dizzy.

Still staring at the sky, I don't know how long I lay there, as my brain slowly began to work again.  I reflected: What now; what will happen now? The deal with Josef was gone. What will happen with me now?

Would I lose everything? Was my career over?

I thought: *The brakeman failed at one sharp curve and the cars left the track and were crushed.*

The last picture in my mind was me as a kid, sitting in the front car screaming for pleasure, enjoying the thrill of the ride. I saw my parents and my brother standing below and watching me on the ride.

Then I passed out.

# Waking Up

*Really great—two pair of jeans, two shirts, one sweater,
and 2,000 dollars. That's it!*

It was like a cold shower hitting me, but it was my beautiful seat
mate next to me on the plane, trying to wake me up. I tried to
jump up like I was fucking crazy, and I realized I was sweating
and felt tears running down my face.

Immediately I remembered the last scene with Josef and it
seemed like it was happening again.

She looked at me and said, "Oh my God, are you okay?"

I said, "I'm sorry; I'm fine. I was wrapped up in a bad dream
... actually, experiencing a bad happening in my past."

"That was really scary; it was like you were fighting for your
life."

"Yes, it was close to that, at least in my dream. I'm sorry, I
didn't mean to bother you. But now that I am awake and over

OH GOD, I THOUGHT. WHAT WAS I WALKING INTO? — my nightmarish dream, may I offer you a drink after scaring the hell out of you.

"That's not necessary, really."

"Please allow me that favor." I waved to the stewardess and she came immediately. My lovely neighbor ordered champagne and I a Jack and Coke.

She told me her name was Sophia and, as I guessed, she was originally from Italy. Under normal circumstances, I would "hit hard" on her, but I had much too much on my mind and was still under the influence of my last dream about Josef.

But still, in my imagination, I wondered how it would be to have a romance or, better yet, wild sex with her. The more I looked at her, the more attractive and sexy I thought she was. I really had to force my mind in another direction—so I started to make small conversation. I told her I was on my way to a new life and a new challenge and then the captain announced our approach into Houston.

I sat up straight in my seat, closed my eyes and thought: *Oh my God, what is going to happened now?* A couple of minutes later the airplane hit the runway and I was ready for my future. I took my luggage and thought: *Really great—two pair of jeans, two shirts, one sweater, and 2,000 dollars. That's it! And what the fuck, I couldn't speak or understand the language either.*

That's the start in my new world. I couldn't stop thinking about all my designer clothes that were left in Austria, all my expensive paintings on the wall by famous painters, all the other expensive shit I bought, and now I had nothing. But, I had to force my mind in another direction. When I passed the nice stewardess, I gave her a hug and she wished me the best, and on my way to the exit

I stopped and gave Sophia a hug, too. She was taking another flight to Miami where she would meet her husband for a short vacation.

I thought that would be nice, but I was headed to customs and a long wait in line.

I hoped Manfred Goss was here to pick me up. I was definitely anxious. I knew my English was a mess. I could hear people talking around me, but the sounds and accents were nothing at all like I'd heard before. The reality was, I couldn't understand one fucking word. This was not English to me at all. The English that I was used to hearing in Monaco sounded totally different.

Oh God, I thought. What was I walking into? I tried to think positively and not let fear take me. I knew deep down in myself that I had only one chance at this new future. I had to be totally positive and strong or it would be the end of my story.

After passing through customs, I thought:

*Okay, Houston, here I am. I swore to myself that whatever I had to do, I would make it happen. I would succeed. I would be on top again. All I had to do was get a ticket for my roller coaster ride. I had to find a ticket to get back in the game. I had to do it for my son and for all those people who tried to destroy me. I had to prove I'm not a loser; I had to prove I'm a fighter.*

*I remembered what a friend of mine said a long time ago—"Falling down is not a shame, but not standing up again is one!"*

When I stepped onto American soil, my fighter attitude returned. I knew I was born to be an entrepreneur and failure was never a reason to quit. I was ready to take on the challenge.

In this moment, I felt deep in my heart, I was ready again for ...

*THE THRILL OF THE RIDE.*

# Acknowledgments

First, to Tony Robbins. His CD series *Power Talk* inspired me with his interview with Frank Kern. Frank explained there how he became a self-made multi-millionaire by selling products on the Internet. Thank you, Frank—your interview helped me greatly.

Second, to my son, Philipp. We had just opened up a hand car wash and it had rained every day since the opening. I was depressed and afraid of losing my business almost before I had launched it. Philipp and I were listening to Tony's CD when he said to me, "Dad, you should write a book. With what you have accomplished in the past, you should write a book about your life. I promise you, you will eventually become a millionaire. You are amazing, you need to tell your story."

Write a book? Not so easy. When I came to America in 1997, I could not speak one word of English. I was born and raised in Vienna, Austria ... where I spoke fluent German, not English. Now, nine years later, I speak okay English, but my writing, well, it needs a little help—an understatement.

But I continued to listen to that CD again and again. And, to get rid of my bad weather syndrome from the startup car wash and the fear of failing, I said to myself, *What the hell can I lose?* I talked to my wife, Megan, and told her my idea. I told her I would move to my yacht and would live there while writing my story. She looked at me with a look and comment I knew well: "Really ..." but she knew that when I made a decision and had a vision, nobody could stop me.

I followed the advice of Frank Kern and hired a ghost writer to translate my weird German English into an understandable American English. The ghost writer did a pretty good job but eventually we split up because we differed in our vision for the book. I then started writing myself in 2009, a total of 1,700 pages to create the first draft.

Megan patiently waited during those months ... Thanks, baby, for your patience, support and love for that one year while I was barely at home, living on my yacht, obsessing on writing my life story. When I was not on the yacht, I was working with my son in our car wash business and visiting home only occasionally.

It cost me a ton of money to get to that point where we settled on a concept, and now, five years later, with some tweaking and editing, my first book is finished.

Many things have happened in my life since finishing what is now my first book. My story is not finished—more books are to come—there's much more to my story after I arrived in America.

I called different publishers but there was no contract or offer I felt comfortable with. Then Megan called one day and told me that she found a website called "The Book Shepherd" with Judith Briles, and I contacted her immediately. It was my lucky day. I really can say, she was and is "The Good Book Shepherd"; she earned that title. I never had the feeling she took advantage of me as a total "Greenhorn." No—the opposite happened. She treated me like I was a professional writer, building a platform of trust with me. I also can say that she charged me more than fairly. Thanks, Judith.

Also, my thanks to Nick Zelinger who created my cover and interior—his openness to my ideas and his flexibility and expertise were much appreciated.

As you now know, writing is not my profession. I write only for three reasons. First, to put my thoughts about my past in order. Second, I think you, my reader, can learn from my story. And third, I don't want to die with a "Bucket List" that was never "emptied"—I believe in living life! When I move to the next level of life I will have nothing on my page of what I think I missed. I did it all! It contains every important point of a life: Love, Success, Failure, New Beginning and finally, the most important thing, *never, never quit dreaming.*

Walt Disney said, "As long as you can dream it, you can achieve it." I've embraced that idea, and I live it.

As to my story, many names have been changed. I'm not out for revenge or to hurt anyone, just to tell my story. At the end of the day, I may have made myself look better and sometimes worse than I deserve, depending on the memory of my feelings at the time.

Often, when I look back, it seems I may have dramatized a part of the story; sometimes the facts were too hard to believe myself. "I did all that?—I said that?—OMG!"

But believe me, the story truly tells about my experience ... and my life.

Enjoy and God Bless,
Hans Sitter

P.S. Gerhard, know that you saved my life. I love you. You and your place remain in my heart. (Gerhard's Café in Fontvieille in Monaco—it exists still today. Visit him.)

Karli, Siegie, Vick, Christa, Joe and all my old friends and employees, I love you and hope you are doing well. I will never forget you guys.

# About the Author
## Johann "Hans" Sitter

Meet Hans Sitter, a legendary serial entrepreneur who has established and worked in an amazing variety of industries during his decades-long, roller coaster of a career. Trained as a butcher in Austria, he quickly realized that his interests and skills were in quite different areas from "butchering."

He is now in his 60s and the driving force behind one of America's most successful German restaurants. His entrepreneurial spirit led him in his youth first to establish several auto-related businesses. His connections in that industry then led him in broadly different directions: opening game rooms, bars, night-clubs, a car dealership and body shop, operating restaurants and flipping properties.

Inspired by the hit TV series, *Dallas*, he opened a gas station in Austria calling it *DALLAS DISCOUNT*. He dressed his employees as cowboys and got the attention that most companies only dream of. Within a few years, moneys flowed; he prospered and moved his family to a permanent residence in Monaco, where they lived among the rich, super rich and famous.

He then sold all his gas stations and with the proceeds, built a Hotel and Fitness center and a Las Vegas style men's club called "Beverly Hills Club." He then decided to sell that enterprise with the idea of moving to the US and starting a business there. Unfortunately, the buyer landed in jail before completion of the sale and Hans lost the entire business, along with his savings, yacht and apartment in Monaco ... the $3,000,000 owed him ...

everything. On top of his financial losses, there was an arrest warrant issued in Austria for tax evasion, and his wife spurned him for losing everything, leaving him for one of his long-time friends.

With her exit, he lost his family and the daily contact he cherished with his two-year-old son Philipp and their beloved Cavalier King Charles Spaniel, Umberto. His story didn't end there, however. He didn't quit ... he started over ... again.

A close and loyal friend in Monaco bought him an airplane ticket to Houston, gave him $5,000 and begged him to leave, to follow his original plan and start over again in America.

Bidding good-bye to a life he loved, he arrived in Houston, Texas, in September of 1996 with a little cash, two pairs of jeans and shoes and a few shirts. The English language was unknown to him. He knew one person in the States and joined him in Houston. That person eventually introduced him to his future wife, Megan. Soon after, his young son, Philipp, came for a visit and stayed—stepmother Megan became Mom.

Together, they created *SCHMATZ—The best from Vienna ...* he was the cook, Megan, the waitress. Hans never quit, always dreaming big. An observer of all things, he watched everything around him. As his English and his understanding of business in America improved, he recognized the real estate boom happening in Houston, Learning to make 90-day options with a minimum down payment on properties, Hans became the new American cowboy: he loved the thrill of the deal and began to flip real estate, then bought a ranch and bred Longhorns. He tried it all. Nothing could stop him ... he thought.

Then with one wrong decision, his financial pinnacle became a valley and he had to file for bankruptcy in 2005. At least, this time he didn't lose his family. Once again, Hans started over ... this time selling Himalayan Crystal Salt and building with his own hands a spa. Partnering with the friend, they bought a property and opened up a hand car wash. It worked, but he was bored and doubly frustrated when it rained, delaying the development of the business. Hans needed more.

He and his son, Philipp, began listening to CDs created by Tony Robbins, particularly the *Money Masters* series with Robbins interviewing millionaire Frank Kern who shared making his first million using a ghost writer. The light bulb went off when Philipp said, "Dad you should write a book. Your life story is as good as that of Frank Kern, You could be a millionaire again." With that, Hans started to write and, with help, put it all together. *The Last Days in Monaco* is the result and is just the first—there are three more books coming!

That same year, they built a restaurant next to the car wash: *King's Biergarten and Restaurant*. Over three years, it has expanded to 75 employees and over 300 seats. And in that three year period, restaurant revenues grew from $800,000 to in excess of $3,000,000. It has been awarded the Best German Restaurant designation in 2012-2013-2014 by *GermanDeli.com* and is consistently recognized as a Top Ten Restaurant for Service in Houston. As multiple reviewers have stated, "It's a hidden gem in Pearland, Texas."

In 2017, Texans welcomed its second restaurant under Hans Sitter's brand and watchful eye. Kings Bierhaus–The Heights opened to rave reviews in Houston. As soon as the doors opened in April, over 10,000 likes hit its Facebook page!

TODAY, Hans remains happily married to Megan and his key business partner is his son, Philipp, who is now the Director of Operations and Marketing of King's Biergarten & Restaurant.

Texans frequently see him in commercials on TV and he and the restaurant are often profiled within the media.

In his 60s, if you asked Hans if he plans on retiring, you will get a big smile and the response, "My hobby and my life intend for me to continue to be an Entrepreneur. I still enjoy THE THRILL OF THE RIDE and retirement would be for me, the death penalty. It would be like forbidding me to breathe and who in the hell wants to stop breathing and be dead?"

From rags to riches to rags and back to riches, Johann "Hans" Sitter is the classic serial entrepreneur. Provocative, engaging, a visionary ... he's like a lightning rod in your presence.

**KingsBiergarten.com**
**Facebook.com/KingsBiergarten**

**KingsBierhaus.com**
**Facebook.com/BierhausHeights**

You've enjoyed *The Thrill of the Ride;*
now read how it all started with
*The Last Days in Monaco.*

## Coming Soon:
*The Careless Gondolier*
Book Three in *The Entrepreneur* series